REDBOOK's

500 Great Dates

Lisa Sussman

REDBOOK's

500
GreaT
DaTes
Creative Fun and Sexy
Ways to Spend Time Together

LISA SUSSMAN

HEARST BOOKS
STERLING PUBLISHING CO., INC.
NEW YORK, NEW YORK

ACKNOWLEDGMENTS

SPECIAL THANKS go to Jacqueline Deval of Hearst Books and to Alison Brower, Jeannie Kim, and Stacy Morrison of REDBOOK magazine not only for the opportunity to write this book but also for making it better with their thoughtful (and often witty) edits, comments, and ideas.

I'm indebted to Marnie Potash, Ed.D., who has been my trusty guide for many years to the crazy wonderful why's of men, women, and romance, as well as to Doctor Darts, Fast Larry, the folks at Coleman, and Robin Forman for their patience when it came to explaining their alien worlds to me.

A huge hug as well to all my friends (and hopefully you still are) and those strangers who cheerfully bared their souls and worst and best dating experiences, tips, and thoughts.

I would also like to thank my unofficial (and unpaid) researcher, Sy Sussman (who also happens to be a wonderful father), and my official (but also unpaid) sitter/mother, the fabulous Lorraine Sussman, who always drops everything when deadlines are looming. The usual kisses to Steven, Jazz, and Tasha, who have been my research mice on many a date and lived to tell the tale. I owe you a date!

Copyright © 2007 by Hearst Communications, Inc.

Library of Congress Cataloging-in-Publication Data
Sussman, Lisa, 1961-
   Redbook's 500 great dates : creative, fun & sexy ways to spend time together / Lisa
Sussman.
      p. cm.
   Includes index.
   ISBN-13: 978-1-58816-562-6
   ISBN-10: 1-58816-562-0
   1. Dating (Social customs) I. Title. II. Title: 500 great dates. III. Title: Five hundred
great dates.
   HQ801.S945 2007
   306.73--dc22

                                    2006032172

10 9 8 7 6 5 4 3 2 1

Book design by Barbara Balch

Published by Hearst Books
A Division of Sterling Publishing Co., Inc.
387 Park Avenue South, New York, NY 10016

Redbook and Hearst Books are trademarks of Hearst Communications, Inc.

www.redbookmag.com

For information about custom editions, special sales, premium and corporate
purchases, please contact Sterling Special Sales Department at 800-805-5489
or specialsales@sterlingpub.com.

Distributed in Canada by Sterling Publishing
^c/o Canadian Manda Group, 165 Dufferin Street
Toronto, Ontario, Canada M6K 3H6

Distributed in Australia by Capricorn Link (Australia) Pty. Ltd.
P.O. Box 704, Windsor, NSW 2756 Australia

Manufactured in China

Sterling ISBN 13: 978-1-58816-562-6
        ISBN 10: 1-58816-562-0

contents

INTRODUCTION

IF YOU THINK dating's just for singles, then you're short-changing your guy, your relationship, and *yourself,* because having regularly scheduled date nights with the man in your life can keep you two close and connected for years to come. Yes, you've probably heard this advice before, but listen up: It's not about having the fanciest date or the most expensive or elaborate one. Date nights work their magic simply by giving you a chance to catch up with each other and shut out the noise of your busy lives. You get to remind yourselves of why you fell in love and how much you still enjoy spending time together. You feed your love and keep it strong.

Of course, the last thing you want is for date night to become a chore or a dull, "not dinner-and-a-movie again!" routine. That's where this guide comes in. We've collected more than 500 hot, fun, date-night ideas: Some are romantic and sexy; others are silly and whimsical. There are dates you can throw together at the last minute, dates that don't cost a dime, even dates you can have without leaving the house. (And forget that old excuse, "We can't get a sitter!"—we've got ideas for that, too.)

So grab your calendar right now and ink in a date for you and him. Then read on, and get inspired!

—The Editors of REDBOOK

Chapter 1

DATE
EXPECTATIONS

Y ou'd think by the time you're a couple and possibly have a child or three under your belt, you'd be able to handle the intricacies of going out for the night with your partner. After all, wasn't that part of the allure of becoming a "we": knowing that you would be able to leave the whole dating game and its high-anxiety "rules" behind? And it is true that you no longer have to worry about getting a first date, let alone a second, when you are waking up daily with the love of your life. All that free-floating anguish and ago-nizing over who pays, what to talk about, whether you should sleep with him—ancient history.

But dating for married couples or for couples who have been together for a long time comes with its own his-and-her matching set of pressures. You no longer have the same time and energy to make sure you have five minutes together without interruption, let alone set aside an entire evening to dote on each other. So when the stars are finally aligned—you've cleared your calendars, you found someone not on "America's Most Wanted" to look after the kids, and there are no playoffs or season finales scheduled—you want the evening to be perfect. Which practically begs for a Murphy's Law moment.

Don't sweat it. You can avoid dating disaster by following these simple save-the-date guidelines:

✔ Make sure that at least every other date gets you out of the house and away from your daily life.

✔ Plan ahead. Once in a while, it's fun to be spontaneous, but if you always leave everything to the last minute, you more often than not end up either doing the same thing over and over or compromising on what you want to do because you don't have reservations, tickets, or a sitter. The more thought you put into your date, the better it comes out—and the better the reward when you get home.

✔ Be clear about who is doing what planning-wise or you may end up doing nothing. At the same time, have an idea of each other's preferences. Things go awry when one of you expects the night to be wine and roses and the other just wants to grab a Dunkaccino and watch the sunset from the mall parking lot. "I don't really want to get all revved up when we go out," says Madge, forty-four. "I just want to relax and reconnect. My husband Elliot would rather go to a club and listen to music. But he would never choose a place where the sound system is so loud that we can't hear each other talk."

✔ Don't act like his mother and be in charge of all the details. Take turns organizing the date. So what if he doesn't know the sitter's number or has no clue which restaurant just got the best review? This isn't about planning the perfect evening; it's about having time with the person you love so you can rediscover, talk, laugh, and enjoy each other. In that context, even eating an overdone chicken at an American Legion banquet can be lovely. Here, four no-hassle ways to divvy up the responsibilities:

1. Designate a goofy heart pillow (or any other over-the-top romantic household item) "it." Take turns passing "it" back and forth. Whoever has "it" is in charge of planning every detail of the date.

2. Both of you scribble half a dozen date ideas on individual scraps of paper (try to be as creative as possible: going to the bookstore to buy a book you can read together, giving each other foot rubs, making a *cordon bleu* meal together . . .). Put the scraps in a bowl. Take turns choosing (the chooser is automatically the planner).

3. If you're both competitive by nature, turn your dates into a Can You Top This? game and go all out on the details. For example, if he planned a romantic night out at your favorite dine-by-candlelight restaurant, you can start with the restaurant on your night but then up the lust ante by redecorating your bedroom with silk sheets, a bottle of chilled something, and scented candles to keep things heated once you return home.

4. Work as a tag team. Get a local magazine and highlight all the things that interest you. Pick whatever activities overlap (i.e., you both marked a music-theater show) as your date and then divide up the tasks of buying tickets, getting a sitter, organizing the food, and whatever else may need to be done to make the date happen.

✔ Be flexible. Even the best-laid plans can go awry and sometimes the alternative can be even more fun, as Liz, forty-four, discovered when the movie she and her husband, Jeff, wanted to see was sold out. "We went clothes shopping at the mall instead," she says. "I can't really say why it was so much fun except that it was unexpected. Jeff always picks good clothes for me."

✔ Face each other. You don't want every date to be the kind that has you sitting side by side;—you need to occasionally be face to face so you can make meaningful eye contact while chatting.

✔ Create your own personal romantic dating rituals together to help short-cut you both straight into an intimate frame of mind. Here, some easy get-connected gestures that never get old:

- Lighting a scented candle when getting ready for your date

- Putting on some romantic tunes, relaxing with a refreshing cocktail (try a Love Me Tender: combine 1 ounce of orange vodka, ½ ounce of raspberry liqueur, and ½ ounce of cranberry juice; shake and pour over ice; strain into a shot glass and share)

- Giving each other a one-minute kiss before you leave the house

- Using old-world manners (he kisses your hand, helps you on and off with your coat, opens the car door for you, and pulls out your chair at the restaurant)

- Holding hands as much as possible

- Taking a shower or bath together when you get home, especially if you slowly wash each other from head to toe

- Writing a post-date "I-had-a-great-time-last-night" e-mail or note

✔ Travel together if possible (leaving in separate vehicles kills the closeness you've spent the whole evening building up).

✔ Leave the Blackberry at home. No cell-phone calls allowed either (unless they're from the sitter or alarm company).

✔ Crank up the car stereo just like you used to.

✔ Don't drink and date. Yes, it's nice to kick back and relax with a few drinks, but nothing will kill an evening faster than feeling fuzzy-headed.

✔ Talk about something other than what the kids did today, extended family issues, car payments, insurance renewals, mortgage points, and the like. While these are important and necessary topics, make a specific nondate time to powwow about them. Otherwise, your romantic rendezvous may begin to resemble a business meeting or—since studies list money, parenting, and in-laws along with sex as the top causes of marital conflict—a shouting match.

One of the defining characteristics of a date is that it creates space for you to move out of your everyday language and converse intimately. The more you date and the more new and different dates you try, the more opportunity you will have to talk, and the more things you will have to talk about. There is always something new to discover about each other. You just need the time to find out what it is.

One more thing: Don't underestimate the power of shutting up occasionally. Listening is also sexy. Most of us will perk up our ears to compliments and sexual requests, but we're not so good at really tuning in to each other's day-to-day stuff. Sometimes, when you've been together for a while, you develop conversational clairvoyance: You think you know what the other person is going to say, so you zone out. But here is what happens when you really give each other your full attention: You become the most important thing in each other's worlds. You feel warm and gooey inside as you look tenderly into your lover's eyes. You don't just hear the words; you hear the emotions behind what you are both saying. When you are truly listened to, your mind starts to open up, your feelings open up, and your heart opens up.

✔ Have the courage to change your expectations. Don't lower them; change them. It's easy to get stuck in the ideal of what your date night can be: full of romance, love, excitement, rapport, and amazing sex. But when your expectations of date night are unrealistic, you set yourself up for coming crashing down over the smallest things: The food was too salty. The movie was silly. He didn't get my joke. Rigid expectations can blind you to the fact that all you need is you, him, and some free time to connect.

✔ While it would be nice, don't make wild sex the goal of your date. Although an exclusive redbookmag.com poll on your date-night deeds showed that 70 percent of you are ending your evening in a bedtime romp, the main reason for making this time together is to create a chunk of time when you can give each other your undivided attention.

YOUR GET-IT-ON DATELINE

Face it: You may have circled the day on the calendar, made arrangements for childcare, picked out an outfit, and even made reservations, but that doesn't guarantee that you'll be in the mood to snap into date-diva mode once your date night rolls around. Sometimes, after a hard week, you'd sooner slip into some comfy clothes and veg out on the sofa than put on the ritz with your husband. Here, your countdown to getting in the date groove.

• Three Things to Do Right This Minute •

Lose the excuses and consider these think-ahead moves.

1 *Start a date jar.* After putting money aside for the necessities of life like mortgage payments, medical bills, food, car expenses, and so on, put a small amount into the jar, whatever you feel you can comfortably afford. You'll be surprised how quickly it adds up ($1.00 a day equals the cost of a bottle of vino, a bottle of massage oil, a bar of excellent chocolate, or a couple of scented candles by the end of the week). This will take care of any we-can't-afford-to-date ploys (you can also check out the dirt-cheap alternatives listed under "Real-Steal Deals" throughout the book).

2 Get in the habit of picking up your local listings paper or accessing it online. (Most areas have an events site; google the largest nearby town and "events" or "calendar.") This is an easy way to get up-to-date on all sorts of unusual (and often free) goings-on in your area, plus you'll find out if anything hot is in the works in case you need to purchase tickets in advance or make reservations.

3 If possible, pay before you go. It's the law of coupon cutters everywhere: If you've already put up the dough for an event, you're much more likely to follow through no matter how draggy your mood. Happy bonus: knowing you have set-in-stone plans that night will keep you in a state of date expectancy. Check into cultural programs such as concert or theater groups that offer a series of three or more shows. These events often include special perks like lectures or drinks and appetizers on the night of the show as well as discounts on ticket purchases.

• Three Must-Do Things to Do the Week Before Your Date •

It's never too early to start building anticipation for your special night.

1 Get pumped by sending each other "I can't wait until [the date night] rolls around" e-mails, text messages, or phone calls. Describe what you're planning to do (be as X-rated as you dare), what you are going to wear, or how much you're looking forward to spending some quality time together. Or send a notice via sendomatic.com, a free service that lets you create your own event invitation.

2 Stock up on love tunes to keep in your car so you can hit a sentimental high note the moment you leave the house. If you arrive at your destination in the middle of a song, sit and make out until the last beat sounds.

3 Shower him with love. These three retro gift goodies are guaranteed to put him in a just-the-two-of-us mind-set. Think of them as your dating toolbox.

- **FLOWERS.** *Everyone* loves a floral offering (even your husband). Give a single rose or a large bouquet (1800FLOWERS.com, FTD.com, and 1–800–SEND –FTD are nationwide and offer same-day delivery service).

- **CANDY.** You don't need to go gourmet; his favorite chocolate bar is enough to start the night on a sweet note.

- **STUFFED ANIMAL.** Sure, it's hokey, but that's the point: You don't have to spend a lot. Pick up a cuddly toy at a dollar store.

• Seven Things to Try in the Hour Before Your Date •

It's hard to switch into a love-to-love-you mood after you've been on the go all day. Luckily, it doesn't take much to reboot. Here are some low-energy strategies to help you get jazzed—instantly—for the night ahead.

1 If your children come in size small, chances are your date-night prep includes waving your mascara wand while you help find a misplaced teddy, dry tears, and make a quick kid-friendly snack. Stop the madness! Instead, have the sitter come a little early so you and your sweetie can muster at your leisure, preferably while sipping a very chilled glass of white wine.

2 Take a fifteen-minute pretend nap. Since energy tends to plummet in late afternoon, use this time to turn down the lights, turn off the phone, and close your eyes. You may initially feel fuzzy when you reopen your eyes, but you'll soon feel a power surge.

3 Take a breather. More than food, oxygen is the gas that your body runs on. Inhaling deeply is like filling your body with fuel. Take a deep measured breath through your nose, hold for one count, then exhale slowly through your mouth. Repeat five times. You'll feel refreshed and ready for your night.

4 Get a quick adrenalin shot with this simple yoga move: Bend at the waist and hang your head down so that your hands are touching your toes (or are in the general vicinity) and you're looking at your knees. Relax your upper body. Hold this position for several seconds, then slowly rise. Repeat four more times.

5 Skip the coffee and soda; chocolate will give you the jolt you need (yummy!). Pep things up by indulging in some sinfully sexy truffles that you can feed to each other as you gear up.

6 Take a stimulating shower. Use a loofah or soap scented with refreshing oils like tea tree or lemon. While you're in there, make a little mood music of your own and sing as loud as you can (the tile acoustics make even the froggiest croaker sound smooth).

7 Give yourself a tune-up with these three musical moves.

- Turn your favorite dance music on loud and do jumping jacks or a step routine or just dance around. All it takes is ten minutes to get your blood pumping.

- While you're getting ready, listen to your own energizing sound track. If you have the equipment, shuffle your CDs for a four-song progression of selections. Start with something quiet and cool (such as Erykah Badu or Van Morrison). Next, choose something a little faster and louder (try for an early strut-your-stuff Rolling Stones or The Strokes). Third, go for an upbeat, slightly raucous tune (choose something like Prince, Christina Aguilera or Beyoncé). Last, think revvy and boppy: some R&B to shake you out the door (Marvin Gaye, Aretha Franklin, Kanye West, or Joss Stone). You'll be groovin' and movin' at your dressing table.

- Dance in your date. Put on a favorite slow song, snuggle up, and sway to the beat. Don't talk; connect through touch and eye contact. The entire night will suddenly have a richly romantic tone.

•Fast Fixer-Uppers for Twenty Minutes Before Your Date•

Instead of speeding through your get-ready moves, enjoy getting dolled up. Try at least one of these pampering ploys:

- Share your shower, but don't take one together, unless elbowing each other to get under the shower spray is your idea of date foreplay. Instead, overlap so one of you is getting in as the other is getting out. This will give you just enough time for a naked hug. Now *that's* a steamy way to warm up for your date!

- Put your tired feet in stiletto condition with this quick refresher: Buff bare feet with an exfoliating paddle, such as a LaCross Smooth-It Foot Wand (around $3.50 from most drugstores); then soak feet in warm water for two minutes, remove and towel dry, and rub in a scented cream like Dr. Scholl's Pedicure Essentials Cooling Peppermint Lotion (around $5.00 from drugstores). Now lie back and put your feet up for ten minutes.

- Skip the panty hose (and the underwear if you dare).

- "Forget" to button an extra button on your blouse. Then, during the evening, slowly run your finger down your neck to draw his eye down, down, down.

- Invite your honey to choose your outfit, from underwear to jewelry. If you're worried about his sense of style (or lack thereof), make the offer on a night you are going to a place where the lighting is low.

- Getting ready separately will bring back those pre-marriage dating days before he had ever seen you without makeup, let alone rolling on the deodorant. So close the bathroom door, primp, and then parade your gorgeous self out the door minutes before it's time to leave.

- Get decked out every once in a while. Even if you're just going to the local diner, slip into your most glamorous duds (and have him do the same). There is nothing more surefire than looking like your best version of yourself to make the evening feel special and inspire connection (and passion).

- If your outfit closes in the back, let him do you up. It's somehow retro and hot all at the same time.

- You don't have to slip into a micromini to make a sexy statement. True vixen vamping is all about feeling comfortable in what you are wearing.

  1. Wear something ordinary in an unexpected way: Wear a long beaded scarf as a belt, slip on a man's oversized white shirt unbuttoned as a wrap-around shirt, use a suit jacket as a sexy smart shirt, or combine something girly and gauzy with something sexy and tight.

  2. Wear just one dramatic piece of jewelry: shoulder-duster earrings, an eye-catching necklace, a handful of bangles, an ankle bracelet, or a brightly colored ring.

  3. Wear jeans with heels to instantly glamorize a casual look.

  4. Make a grand exit. Sexy is all about surprises, so a deceptively simple dress from the front can be a showstopper in the back. Open backs, lace-up backs, great dress trains all make for dramatic effects.

5. Be touchable. Cashmere, silky satin, buttery soft suedes will make him want to stroke you.

6. Apply the One-at-a-Time rule. If you decide to show off your legs, try not to flash too much cleavage. If you want to show off your cleavage, then remember not to reveal too much leg. Leave something to his imagination.

7. Think pink for your lips. It feels less risqué than red yet still screams sex. For a grown-up rather than girly shade, look for a deep pink and wear it with little or no other makeup.

8. Instead of a daring scoop-neck top, draw his eye to your cleavage subtly with a sparkly trim or necklace.

9. When you need to be dressed to kill in ten minutes or less, instantly glam up your look with a scarf. Use it as a hairband à la Grace Kelly, wear it around your waist instead of a belt, wrap it around your neck, or let it hang loose over your shoulders. If it is big enough, it can even double as a bold top by wrapping it crosswise over your chest. Look for scarves with a sweet fringe, jeweled trim, or in bright bold colors to help make your fashion statement.

Try these four oh-so-sexy ways to help him get ready:

1 Give him a close shave: Have him lean back in a comfortable chair (put some towels on the floor to help with clean up). Slightly moisten a towel and heat it for no more than forty-five seconds in the microwave (any longer and the heat will burn him), then wrap it around his face and neck for a minute to soften his stubble. Remove the towel and rub his face and neck with a few drops of preshave oil (a little goes a long way toward warming his skin, softening his beard, and helping the shaving cream adhere and stay moist longer). Let the oil sit for a few minutes and then slather on shaving cream or lotion, using a circular motion to help raise the hairs for a smoother cut. Using a clean, sharp blade, start shaving. Work from the neck up in long smooth strokes, going in the same direction as the hair growth. Reapply shaving cream and shave lightly against the grain. Once you've finished, repeat the hot-towel routine, then finish with a cold one to close pores and perk him up. End with a massage of aftershave lotion to make him feel spoiled and refreshed. (You can pick up kits of preshave oil, shaving lotion, and aftershave cream for around $50 from drugstores or online. Anthony Logistics for Men and Nivea products are good for all skin types.)

2 Tie his tie for him. To make the classic four-in-hand knot, hang the tie around his neck, with the narrow end hanging down on his right side and the wide end hanging down a little longer on his left. Cross the wide end over the narrow end so that it forms a cross. Using your left hand, pinch the crossing point between your thumb and two fingers. Wrap the wide end all the way around behind the narrow end, over your thumb and fingers, and back to the right. Now, bring the wide end up through the V from behind. Push the wide end though the space where your fingers are. Pull it tight (you may have to adjust it). If the narrow end is longer than the wide end, start over. The wide end shouldn't go down any farther than his belt when standing or he'll look like someone's crazy old Uncle Joe.

3 Iron his shirt. There is something about slipping into a crisp, freshly ironed shirt that makes a man stand tall and proud.

4 Put him through prep school. Most men find what they like and stick with it, year in, year out, whatever the current fashions. Here are the absolute basics for a well-built wardrobe that will get him dating in style:

- Five well-made T-shirts that can be worn with a jacket or jeans (no band tours, hardware store advertisements, team logos, or college mascots)
- One all-around suit (other than the ones worn for work) that fits well
- One navy gabardine three-button jacket, which can be worn all year, with anything
- One pair of dark khaki pants, one pair of light-colored chino-style pants, one pair of jeans, all of which are multipurpose
- A crisp white shirt—instant class for any outfit
- Three solid-colored shirts
- One well-made pullover (fine wool or cashmere)

FOR WHEN YOU'RE WALKING (OOPS!) SASHAYING YOUR SEXY SELF OUT THE DOOR

You think because he's your husband, your flirting days are over? Actually, they've just begun, because you can be more outrageous and risqué with the man you live with than you ever could with some stranger. And getting flirtatiously frisky is a surefire way to warm up your private time together, even if you're discussing mundane things like whether the car needs new brakes. So be a sexy babe and bring romance front and center with these make-him-weak-at-the-knees maneuvers.

● Three must-do kisses:

1. Put your long-last lipstick to the test and kick off your night together with a sloppy make-out session, the kind that used to last for hours on end when you were a new couple.

2. Institute a red-light kiss rule: If you're in the car, lean in for a smooch each time you come to a red light and hold it until the light turns green (or someone honks at you!).

3. Get in touch with a full-body hug as you pucker up. Physical contact keeps you emotionally connected and may warm you up for a steamier union later.

- If you're meeting somewhere, try to get there first so you can greet him with a huge hug and a smile. And when you see him coming toward you, don't just walk to meet him; run.

- Hold his hand and don't let go until you have to.

- "Accidentally" brush against him as you walk together.

- Tell him how hot he looks and how you plan to ravish him later.

- Never underestimate the power of a smile, especially when you use it to replace your usual eye roll when he makes his "You often hear of a good wine through the grapevine" pun for the hundredth time.

- Place a suggestive hand on his arm or thigh while sitting in the car.

- Make eye contact. Hold the gaze for just a few seconds longer than usual.

Chapter 2

DInner
AnD a MOVIe

The dinner/movie combo is a bit like the PBJ of dating: your fallback when you haven't organized anything else. According to the redbookmag.com poll, 92.8 percent of you say your regular date consists of dinner and/or a movie. It's not that you don't want to try new things, but by the time your date night rolls around, it can seem like too much of a hassle to do anything more than head out for a quick bite before checking out the latest four-star release.

One little thing: Mixing things up is what keeps your movie date feeling interesting and new. The funny thing is, we strive for comfort in our relationships, but then we get too much of a good thing and become complacent about finding new ways to crank up the thrills.

In the beginning, things were interesting without effort, sort of a gift from the universe. Now, however, if you want it to continue to be interesting, you are going to have to make it so.

Luckily, it doesn't take much to freshen up the food-and-flick night out. All of the ideas below are guaranteed to jolt you out of your amour apathy and maybe even offer a few opportunities to steal a kiss without getting popcorn stuck in your teeth.

TEN MUST-DO DINNER-AND-A-MOVIE UPDATES

Pull these switcheroos on your regular meal-and-movie dates. You may not want (or be able) to do them every time the urge hits to visit the silver screen, but aim to try at least one of these every third time you go to the movies to keep private time together endlessly fascinating.

1 Skip the trip to the megaplex. Sure, it may have seventeen screens and stadium seating, but going to a movie at one of these monsters is a bit like going to a cattle call, especially on a weekend night when the place turns into teen party scene. Some smaller cinemas have sofas or lift-up arm rests (airplane style) so you can snuggle up while you watch the action (and perhaps make some of your own). And the more mature viewing matter means you don't have to worry about your babysitter catching you necking during the previews.

2 Try a restaurant/movie theater combo. Picture this: You're enjoying a nice meal at your favorite restaurant when you look down at your watch and realize that in order to make your nine P.M. movie, you're going to have to scarf the rest of your food, skip dessert, and drive like a NASCAR competitor across town to make it on time. If this sounds familiar, a restaurant/cinema may be just the ticket. Some offer dining before the movie by working dinner seatings around show times, while others will serve food and drinks during the film.

3 Skip the blockbuster. Instead, try these surprise movie genres to stir up a lovey-dovey mood:

- **HORROR FILMS:** Grab each other and hold on tight for comfort and security during the scream scenes.

- **HEAVY INTELLECTUAL FILMS WITH COMPLI-CATED PLOTS:** Stop trying to figure out what the hell is going on and make out instead.

- **FOREIGN FILMS:** Let the romantic accents woo you into a sexy daze.

- **COMEDIES:** There is nothing like unwinding together with a laugh to put you on the same blissful wavelength.

4 Become a movie critic. Libraries and colleges often host movie and discussion nights.

5 Check out IMAX. With their huge screens and occasional 3-D action, IMAX theaters are just what you need to quickly add a new dimension to your movie experience. And because they're rarely longer than an hour, you don't even need to make a night of it, that is, unless you want to. Check out *www.imax.com* for a theater location near you.

6 Turn your night into a mini vacation by matching your menu to your movie: if you're seeing the latest kung fu action flick, get some spicy noodles at your local Chinese restaurant; for French films, go to an intimate neighborhood bistro; if it's an Italian family drama, share a bowl of spaghetti. Or turn your dinner into foreplay when you go to eat one of these sexy spreads:

- **CHEESE OR CHOCOLATE FONDUE** (often served at French or Swiss restaurants). There's something erotically decadent about dipping bits of food into a gooey rich sauce and licking your sticky fingers. Feeding each other drippy forkfuls will raise your meal rating from PG to R.

- **SEAFOOD:** caviar, oysters, lobster, etc. These foods practically spell *sex* (as long as you don't have a food allergy). Despite their luxurious aura, you really don't need to have an extra $1,000 in your wallet to indulge. A good seafood restaurant will often have a wide price range of these foods on the menu. The less expensive choices are still going to pack every bit of the same lusty punch as their pricier counterparts.

- **MOROCCAN FOOD.** You tend to sit side by side on a pile of cushions, eat with your hands, and may even get to watch a belly dancing show. How's that for lust on the menu?

- **JAPANESE.** Check out the movie *Tampopo* if you think slurping noodles can't be sexy. Some Japanese restaurants have private rooms where can you get up close and cozy, seated on tatami mats on the floor.

- **INDIAN.** The hot, spicy ingredients are said to get your blood pumping and give your libido a lift.

7 Instead of going out on one movie date, guarantee yourself around twenty-five dates in a row by getting a season's worth of your favorite TV show on DVD and watching it together every night. Notch up the romantic mood by finding a collection of a TV show that was popular when you became a couple. Or take a trip down memory lane. Pick up some candy that was popular when you were a kid (if it's no longer available in stores, you may be able to find it at hometownfavorites.com) and spend the night watching old home movies. Go ahead and retell the story behind the movie. This is a favorite date for Heather, thirty-four, and her husband: "He never tires of watching the movie of me and my older sister when my mother dressed me as Wilma Flintstone and my sister as a fairy princess for Halloween. What was she thinking? Naturally, I spend the entire movie stealing my sister's wand and bashing her over the head with it. Hence, my husband's nickname for me: Cavewoman Princess!"

8 Some theaters offer inexpensive late-night fright nights or cult-film showings on weekends. Indulge your inner movie star! Some of these movies, such as *The Rocky Horror Picture Show* and *The Sound of Music,* often encourage audience participation where viewers dress up as their favorite characters and perform the movie as it plays.

9 Branch out. Instead of always going to the same-old, same-old restaurant and cineplex, check out what's on offer at your next closest town. Even if the cuisine and movie aren't all that different from what you'd find in your own neighborhood, traveling to a new location will make your date feel shiny new.

10 Laugh like a kid again at the latest G-rated movie (go to a later show when the real tykes are safely home in bed). "It makes me laugh to watch him giggling like some seven-year-old," says one woman who regularly goes to children's movies with her husband. "It makes him more attractive to me because it reminds me of why I fell in love with him: his silly fun side."

Of course, this date might not be such a heart racer if you have small children at home who would be mighty peeved to learn that Mommy and Daddy went to see *Shrek X* without them. In which case, skip the G-rated fare and chuckle over the infectious silly humor of whatever dumb-and-dumber adult slapstick is on offer (generally anything by the Farrelly brothers, Adam Sandler, or Ben Stiller will fit the bill).

PICKUP DATES

No plan? No problem. Here are four last-minute dates, no forethought required.

1 If you have a laptop with a DVD drive, take it out with you. Head to the largest bookstore in your area, purchase a movie you really wanted to but never got around to seeing, order a couple of coffees and some baked sweets at the bookstore café, find a love seat to cuddle up in (if your computer isn't charged, look for one near an outlet), and create your own drive-in experience.

2 If you have a PC, you can get software for around $20 a year (much less than cable costs) that will let you download a wide assortment of movies (moviedirectpro.com and downloaddevil.com are two of the better sites).

3 Turn your home into a movie theater. Lay out a big blanket in your backyard. Fix a cinema-style snack like chips and dip, popcorn, or bowl of Twizzlers. Then bring your TV and DVD or VCR outside and, using a long extension cord, sit back and enjoy the show.

4 When you don't have dinner reservations and haven't pre-purchased your movie ticket, don't assume it's easier to hit the golden arches and then return to your sofa to catch whatever is on TV. Try sitting at the restaurant bar (it's actually the best seat in the house for people watching). Or put a time limit on yourselves: If you cross-your-heart-and-hope-to-die that you are just going to have one quick dish, the maître d' will often try to squeeze you in. Then just go and see whatever film you can get into. After all, it's just a movie, about 105 minutes of your life (or 185 if it's an epic or has been directed by Peter Jackson). Taking even small chances together lets you explore new and exciting sides of yourself and each other. And if the movie is truly awful, it'll give you more to talk about after.

REAL-STEAL DEALS

Going to a movie and dinner can easily add up to $100. These dirt-cheap diversions won't bust your budget.

- Look over your membership perks. Some clubs, professional and alumni institutions, and coupon books offer discounted movie tickets. Then cut the dinner bill with these cost-saving tricks:

  1. Look for a bar that has a happy hour offering two-for-one drinks and free munchies.

  2. For really cheap eats and entertainment, check your local papers for supermarket grand openings and nibble on the free food samples.

  3. Eat like royalty at pauper's prices: Chow down at your local buffet (check the times; many have early-bird specials) or check out a restaurant known for its excessively large portions and share a meal together. But be careful not to overindulge, or you're going to be less in the mood to indulge each other's passions later on.

- During warmer months, many cities offer an alternative to sitting inside a stuffy movie theater with free outdoor screenings. Local libraries and museums also sometimes screen unexpected films, from classics to documentaries. Check schedules in your free city circular.

- Just have coffee instead of a meal. Even though some of the swishier coffee places can break the bank, two grande lattes are still cheaper than a three-course dinner. For around $15, you can both get a caffeine extravaganza complete with whipped cream on top and decadent dessert to share. Sit knee to knee at one of the little round tables that seem to be a design must at these places, lean close together, and share the dessert.

- Skip dinner to leave room for dessert. After the movie, go to the supermarket to pick up the mixings for the biggest, craziest ice cream sundae ever. Share, using one spoon, and take turns passing the cherry back and forth between your mouths.

- Try brunch and a matinee; fancy restaurants are way more affordable in the A.M.

- Make your own movie deal. Some cinemas have cheap midweek nights. Or see if there is a second-run movie house in your area. Because these movies have been in the theaters for a few months, they're about one-third of the price of a newly released film.

- Skip the pricey theater junk food and share an ice cream

cone instead. There is nothing sexier than accidentally touching tongues as you lick up your double dip.

● For dinner and a movie under $5, go to the local library and look over their video selection (some libraries work with other branches and let you preorder a specific title). Then go to the drive-thru at a local fast-food joint and get two meals to take home.

THE RIGHT RENTALS

Not sure what movie you want to rent or having trouble finding a film you'll both like? Try matching the movie to your mood.

● Five all-time top romantic movies for when you want to fall in love with each other all over again (a "**K**" rating means keep the Kleenex handy):

   1. *Casablanca* (1942): A truly perfect love triangle with a bit of war and sophisticated intrigue thrown in. **K**

   2. *Groundhog Day* (1993): Who hasn't fantasized about being able to relive a day until you get it right?

   3. *Truly Madly Deeply* (1991): An intelligent, moving, and deeply funny story about love and death. Think *Ghost* with wit. **K**

   4. *Four Weddings and a Funeral* (1994): An effortlessly enchanting romantic comedy about life, death, and commitment.

5. *Shakespeare in Love* (1998): A passionate, romantic comedy of errors full of mixed-up identities, love gone wrong, smart dialogue, and plenty of lusty moments. Shakespeare would have loved it!

- Three R-rated flicks for when you're too whacked to follow the dialogue (hit the Mute button; you won't miss a thing) and just want to enjoy some sexy visuals:

   1. *Showgirls* (1995): Soft-porn cliché about aspiring—ahem—actresses.

   2. *Wild Orchid* (1990): Sex games in Rio de Janeiro.

   3. *Killing Me Softly* (2002): Two fetching actors (Heather Graham, Joseph Fiennes) and lots of nudity, especially in the unrated version.

- Two macho movies that actually have an absorbing plot:

   1. *Crouching Tiger, Hidden Dragon* (2000): This kung-fu film has no shortage of breathtaking crunch-pow-zap battles, but it also has the elements of a tear-jerking tragedy, the sweep of an epic romance, and a kick-ass female star.

   2. *Master and Commander: The Far Side of the World* (2003): Bristling with swashbuckling he-men, this seafaring adventure is thrilling enough to make a landlubber yearn for the high seas. The only romance is between Russell Crowe and his ship, but what a love story it is!

- Four erotic thrillers that you'll want to watch in bed (for adults only):

    1. *Secretary* (2001): Who thought S&M lite could be erotic and funny?

    2. *Unfaithful* (2002): Yes, it proves that adultery is inevitably destructive, but it also proves that affair sex is scorching stuff!

    3. *Cold Heart* (2000): A sexy albeit frightening reversal of *Fatal Attraction.*

    4. *Basic Instinct* (1992): A suspenseful, cat-and-mouse erotic thriller with psychosexual overtones. Not to mention Sharon Stone doing the no-underwear thing.

- Five chick flicks that he'll love too:

    1. *My Big Fat Greek Wedding* (2002): A smart, down-to-earth hilarious love story including a family that will make you both grateful for your respective in-laws.

    2. *50 First Dates* (2004): He'll love Adam Sandler, and you'll love the story of a man who must prove his love over and over again.

    3. *Sidewalks of New York* (2001): A modern *Annie Hall* without the Woody Allen whine. You'll want to spend your next vacation in the Big Apple.

    4. *Wedding Crashers* (2005): This movie somehow manages to seamlessly mix smart humor with mushy romance and the occasional bawdy joke.

5. *Some Like It Hot* (1959): A delightfully fizzy cross-dressing comedy results when two hapless night-club musicians accidentally witness a mob murder and skip town by dressing up as women and joining an all-female band that includes Marilyn Monroe. 'Nuff said.

- Five guy movies that he'll adore you for choosing and that you won't mind watching (though you might not tell him that):

    1. *Gladiator* (2002): A rousing, grisly, action-packed epic that will leave him marveling at the glory that was Rome and you marveling at the glory that is Russell Crowe.

    2. *Three Kings* (1999): One of the most seriously funny war movies ever made, but if Humvees and the politics of war aren't your thing, you can always ogle the talent: George Clooney and Mark Wahlberg.

    3. *Ocean's 11* (2001): A slick witty plot, sexual intrigue, and a foursome of dishy actors (George Clooney, Brad Pitt, Matt Damon, Don Cheadle) result in a caper as smooth as a Cosmopolitan.

    4. *The Bourne Supremacy* (2004): Much better than Bourne One, this sequel is a well-thought-out spy thriller that puts you right in the thick of the fast-paced action, which hurtles from India to Berlin, Moscow, and Italy.

5. *Spider-Man* (2002): A thoroughly entertaining superhero story with an adorable couple of leads (Tobey Maguire and Kirsten Dunst) who don't make you feel like you haven't been spending enough time at the gym.

- Five classic screwball comedies to have on hand just in case you thought your lives were crazy insane (plus the romance/laugh combo is flat-out sexy):

   1. *It Happened One Night* (1934): A runaway bride and a hard-bitten reporter, a shared hotel room, and just the right amount of sexual tension makes this the perfect feel-good movie.

   2. *Bringing Up Baby* (1938): The pace is frenetic from the get-go and never lets up until airhead heiress Katharine Hepburn and straight-laced scientist Cary Grant overcome every possible obstacle to find love.

   3. *The Awful Truth* (1937): In this quintessential romantic comedy, Cary Grant and Irene Dunne play a young husband and wife who, suspecting each other of having an affair, get divorced and then can't keep away from each other.

   4. *The Philadelphia Story* (1940): A fast-paced plot that strikes the perfect balance of being spectacularly well acted, totally romantic, hysterically funny, and delightfully silly while maintaining an elegant veneer.

   5. *The Thin Man* (1934): William Powell and Myrna Loy play Nick and Nora Charles, a couple of suave married detectives who find each other delightful and who together view life as a goofy martini-laced adventure.

- Two rock-on movies that will have you dancing down the house:

  1. *A Hard Day's Night* (1964): A "typical" day in the life of The Beatles.

  2. *School of Rock* (2003): The world's least-employable heavy metal guitarist poses as a substitute teacher at a prep school and tries to turn his class into a rock band. The fact that the prof is Jack Black makes this a LOL comedy.

- Five violent but widely praised films that will have you talking for days (warning: not for the faint of heart):

  1. *Full Metal Jacket* (1987): Called the "definitive Vietnam film," this movie also manages to be a fresh take on the ethics of war.

  2. *Fight Club* (1999): A modern-day morality play warning of the decay of society as depicted through cold-blooded physical violence

  3. Pretty much anything by Quentin Tarantino will guarantee you a riveting plot full of crosses, double crosses, and triple crosses made edgier with fast-cut editing, witty dialogue, an excellent soundtrack, and copious amounts of blood. Try *Reservoir Dogs* (1992), *Pulp Fiction* (1994), or *Kill Bill, Volume One* (2003) and *Volume Two* (2004).

- Three scary movies that will have you in a close huddle soon as the opening credits roll. Watch them in the dark:

  1. *The Shining* (1980): The story of a man being driven slowly mad gets under your skin and chills your bones . . . and there's no place to hide.

  2. *Seven* (1995): A serial killer forces his victims to die by acting out one of the seven deadly sins, arranging each murder scene into a grotesque graphic illustration of each mortal vice.

  3. *Scream* (1996): A postmodern slasher movie that playfully acknowledges all the exhausted horror clichés and still manages to make your blood run cold.

DATING DILEMMAS

It can be a shock when your plans for a nice quiet night out, eating dinner and watching a movie, turns into your own melodrama. Here's how to plot your night sans tears.

Dilemma #1:
Fighting over what movie to see

He's in the mood for a couple of guys goofing it up; you want a couple of crazy-in-lust lovers smooching it up. You could have a thumb war (winner chooses), or you could be adult about it and agree to take turns. Staying open-minded about each other's interests is one way to keep your relationship strong.

Dilemma #2:

Comparing your love story unfavorably with the one you've just watched

There is nothing like watching two people fall head over heels in perfect love to make you feel lukewarm about your own romantic plot, concedes relationship psychologist Marlin S. Potash, Ed.D., author of *Hidden Agendas* and other books on men, women, and the whole love shebang. But, she is quick to point out, "the characters in these movies get away with behavior that would be odd at best and potential psycho material at worst in real life. The same behavior in your lover would either irritate you or possibly freak you out." So before you think about recasting him, read her expert input on a few classic romantic movies:

- *Sleepless in Seattle:* Everyone has irritating habits, but does that mean you should drop your partner and start stalking some stranger? Also, what man in his right mind would date a woman who went to such a psychotic effort to land him?

- *Jerry Maguire:* If a man has a fear of commitment, it would be nice to think he was just waiting for you to come along to change his fickle ways. But no matter how adorable, loyal, and loving you are, the only thing that makes a commitment-phobe change his colors is figuring out what he is scared of and really, really, really wanting to make things different.

- *When Harry Met Sally:* After enough bad relationships, you may very well fall for your best male friend. But if there has never been any heat between you—a flirty connection that highlighted all your interactions—you are going to feel more like two very good friends living together than two hot-and-heavy lovers who happen to be great pals as well.

- *Titanic:* Folks, it was an archetypal holiday fling! They were from two completely different worlds, knew nothing about one another, and were on the equivalent of a cruise ship. The real trick for the staying power of a relationship isn't how terrific it is on the high seas with perfect weather when you're in carefree holiday mode; it's how well it fares once you are on dry land and back to your real life.

Dilemma #3:

Talking nonstop during the movie, irritating your sweetie and everyone around you

You may think that because it's a date, you must communicate, communicate, communicate. Otherwise, how can you get in tune with each other? Stop worrying and suck on a Raisinette. Yes, it's good to converse and find out how you are both doing beyond your daily "How did your day go?" chat. And yes, again, date nights are a good time to tête-à-tête about your lives. And yes, one more time, it can be a bonding moment to whisper into his ear "Did you see that?" or "I don't get what is going on." But sometimes it's also enough to just sit side by side, leaning your head against his shoulder, to feel close to each other. "Sometimes, we have been going nonstop all week and have barely had time to say hello to each other," says Steven, 45.

"Sitting in the dark and holding hands gets us back in each other's vision without forcing it."

Dilemma #4:
Saturday-night madness—

It can't be helped, but this is *the* night out for the entire world. Families, teenagers, new couples and old all hit the town on Saturday night. You can give the crowds a miss if you avoid any restaurant, bar, or movie that has recently opened. Or just do date night another night.

Dilemma #5:
You can't decide on a cuisine.

Then don't. Avoid an argument by making your chow time an adventure. Many cinemas are located in malls where, often conveniently placed nearby, there is also a food court. So you can turn your meal into an around-the-world food tour that satisfies both of you and still make it to the cinema in time to see the previews.

Dilemma #6:
The movie was not what you thought it would be.

Next time, to find out if a particular film is date-worthy for you, check out films42.com, a site run by a couple who love the movies and rate them for other couples.

romantic dates

A romantic date is more than a prelude to mad tear-your-clothes-off sex. At the very least, romance lifts your relationship out of the mundane. Over time, the buzz of daily life can blur the physical attraction and passionate love that drew you together in the first place. That's when a sparks-flying tryst can remind you that there's still a connection between you that's pure heat and emotion.

At its best, romance can give your love just the right blend of seduction and security. When you plan an amorous evening, it becomes a way of showing not just how well you know and understand each other but also how much you appreciate each other's uniqueness. Who else but your guy would know that you swoon over a plate of chocolate chip cookies tied with a bow, but a bouquet of flowers leaves you cold? These are the intimate details that connect you no matter what else is happening in your lives.

That said, making love can be an expression of these feelings. So when the groundwork for affection has been laid, there's greater likelihood that you both will get passionately, ecstatically, tenderly laid too.

Some believe that romance should just come naturally, and that if it doesn't, something is wrong. Nothing could be further from the truth. Time, coupled with familiarity, is the great destructor of ooey-gooey romance, which is why true romance, the kind that defines a thoughtful and lasting love, is in the actual stoking of the flames. It's in the attention you give your partner and the willingness to start fresh over and over, to learn how to constantly embrace and honor your union.

The following ideas will help you to keep your love connections charged.

TEN MUST-DO DATES
FOR THE ROMANTICALLY
CHALLENGED

Even those who are still swoony in love need a kick in the pants now and then to liven up things romantically. After all, candle-lit dinners and sultry music are only going to get you so far. Happily, it doesn't take much to pack a little lovey-doveyness into your night out. Try these simple yet sexy ways to sweeten up your time together. Try to take your time. Remember: Neither of you has to be anywhere except together.

1 These new and improved tips for the classic romantic dinner date will have you hanging a DO NOT DISTURB sign when you get home:

- Go to a restaurant that has a dance floor. Even if the only music you know how to dance to is the Bunny Hop, you can still wrap your arms around each other and sway to the beat.

- Share a luscious dessert using just one spoon.

- Choose a restaurant that has small tables so that you can't help but rub knees during your meal.

- Surprise your partner by arranging to have a single rose delivered during your meal.

- Take a dinner/dance cruise. The gentle rocking motion of the ocean lulls you into a sensuous mood (think water beds).

2 Don't forget to crank up the flirty moves. If it's been so long that you can't remember, here's a refresher course in seduction:

- Throw him a smoldering, come-hither look: Lock eyes for a full five to six seconds, then smile and drop your gaze. He'll melt on the spot.

- Make yourself irresistibly kissable. If you're drinking something frothy like beer or a latte, take a sip of your drink and slowly lick the foam from your lip with the tip of your tongue.

- Slay him with this seductive move: Start the evening with your hair gathered in a ponytail or clip. Then, when you want to grab his attention and give him a taste of where the evening is going to lead, pull your hair loose and let your tresses cascade around your face.

- Make the most of a loud room and lean in close. Then whisper so he has to lean in even closer.

3 Go to the library or bookstore and pick out a book of romantic poetry to read to each other while cuddling up, preferably naked, in bed. Use your sexiest voice and linger on the more suggestive passages. If you think reading poetry is going to feel too much like high school English (or that you need a British accent to make the words sound believable), then check out *You Drive Me Crazy: Love Poems for Real Life* edited by Mary D. Esselman and Elizabeth Ash Vélez for plain-language verses that cover all the stages of love, whatever your lyrical mood.

4 There is nothing like the unqualified, blatant language of faith that a marriage ceremony contains to make you fall hard in love all over again. If no one you know is about to walk down the aisle, check out tonylovestina.com to see if the play *Tony 'n' Tina's Wedding* is playing nearby. For the price of a ticket, you get to eat, drink, dance, and be part of the action as family or friends of the "bride" or "groom."

5 On your next date, bring a copy of *The Art of Kissing: Book of Questions and Answers* by William Cane and read about different kinds of kisses (like the "vacuum kiss," which is done by sucking the air out of his mouth as you kiss him). Pick your favorites to try out once you get home.

6 Take dance lessons together. Even if you end up stepping on each other's toes, you'll be forced to pay attention to how your bodies move together. Try and avoid dances that don't involve touching (like line dancing). Instead, try learning how to tango, ballroom dance, waltz, or even square dance (you'll need to work together as a team). At the end of the lesson, be prepared for your dancing fool to sweep you off your feet (and straight into bed).

7 Get intimate before your date. Gene, 32, picked up this nifty tip from sex doyenne Dr. Ruth ages ago, and he says it helps him and his wife ease into date mode. "We don't do it every time, but making love prior to going out lets us completely focus on the pleasure of being with each other because it gets rid of the pressure and tension that builds up over whether the evening will or won't end with sex." The bonus:

When you have already made the sexual connection, you may find that you are more physically receptive to each other during your date. Take advantage of this heightened awareness with little touches to keep you bonded, such as caressing each other's fingers, playing footsie under the table, stealing unexpected kisses, and linking arms or gently bumping shoulders as you walk together.

8 Slink your way into a jazz club and let the sultry tunes rule your body. The smoky air practically oozes sensuality.

9 Make a finger-foods-only dinner and feed each other. If you don't feel like cooking, simply cut up an assortment of juicy sexy fruits: mango, papaya, raspberries, and strawberries. Don't refrigerate, as fruit at room temperature has the most pungent aroma and releases the most flavor when placed on the tongue.

After the meal, warm two moistened hand towels in the microwave for twenty seconds. Unroll and slowly wash each other's hands.

10 Instead of a horse-drawn carriage, take a moonlight ride in a rowboat. (Be safe and wear life preservers.)

GOTTA HAVE IT

Yes, it feels like an indulgence to spend money on your date, but occasionally you need to pamper your relationship. Think of it as maintenance rather than luxury. When you make an effort to take special care of

your partnership, you feel less stressed and better able to cope with the challenges of being part of a couple. Besides, it can only do good things for your sex life. Read on for three dates that spare no expense.

1 Steam things up by renting a hot tub for the weekend. You can find one at hottubrental.com for around $300/weekend (plus delivery) or look in the *Yellow Pages* under "Hot-tub and Spa Rentals."

2 Act like kids again in your own private space. For an hour or two, you can rent an ice rink, bowling alley, or swimming pool.

3 Some foods ooze sex appeal. Spoil your palate with these luxury treats (check out foodnetwork.com for buying, using, and serving tips):

- **OYSTERS:** For a sensory feast with no slaving in the kitchen, slurp them raw, straight out of the shell.

- **CAVIAR AND CHAMPAGNE:** It doesn't get much more sophisticated than this classic combo.

- **TRUFFLE OIL:** Said to smell of sex; a little goes a long way.

- **KOBE-WAGYU BEEF:** For the meat-and-potato eater, a melt-in-your mouth steak that won't feel heavy in your stomach when the action moves into the bedroom.

- **SAFFRON:** Its unique seductive flavor can be added to practically any dish.

- **FIRE**: Splash a few tablespoons of heated brandy onto any cream sauce (savory or sweet) and ignite to give your meal the *ooh-la-la* tone of a fine French restaurant.

- **CHOCOLATE**: Chocolate has deeply sensual overtones, lovely sticky undertones, and stacks of phenylethylamine, a natural "bedroom booster." Add a sinfully sweet flavor to your date with one of these five ingredients:

  1. Pop a chocolate truffle into your mouth and then lay a tasty smacker on your honey.

  2. Turn each other into dessert by squirting chocolate syrup on each other and licking it off. (Use old sheets.)

  3. Titillate your senses with a spritz of chocolate perfume. (Try the tasty Tartine et Chocolate Parfum, around $25 for 1/7 ounce.)

  4. Rendezvous at a spa for a chocolate treatment. Facials, baths, massages, and even exfoliations are just a few of the treats available.

  5. Make a day trip to a chocolate factory. Hershey's in Hershey, Pennsylvania, and Scharffen Berger in San Francisco, California, are two of the biggies, but just about any local handmade chocolate shop will give you a peek behind the scenes if you ask nicely!

DON'T FIGHT
THE URGE TO SPLURGE

Try these no-budget, no-hassle moves for five days to stockpile over $100 for a weekend treat.

- Bag your lunch. *Savings:* approximately $25.

- Skip the gourmet java jolt. Instead, BYO morning coffee. *Savings:* approximately $10.

- Instead of the big names, buy store brands. *Savings:* approximately $10.

- Drink tap water instead of bottled water. *Savings:* approximately $5.

- Get a library card and use it to check out CDs, movies, and books for free. *Savings:* approximately $5.

- Skip a week at the grocery store and use all those things that have been taking up shelf space in your pantry and freezer instead. You'll find you can probably feed an average family for at least one week with what you have on hand in the pantry and freezer. *Savings:* approximately $50.

REAL-STEAL DEALS

Romance does not have to cost a lot of money. These shabby-chic dates only feel high priced.

- It's mood, not food, that sets the romantic scene. If going out to an expensive restaurant isn't an option, you can easily transform dinner from your local fast-food spot into a fancy eating experience. All it takes is a few tiny adjustments to the atmosphere. Bring the food home, and instead of eating it straight out of the bag, set out a tablecloth, a vase with flowers, elegant stemware, your nicest dishes and cutlery. Pour your drinks into your wineglasses (clear soda resembles sparkling wine) and unwrap your food onto your dishes. *Bon appétit!*

● You don't need to choose between a sumptuous feast and making a car payment. This simple shoestring menu will bring back those heady infatuated-with-each-other days of dating when a splurge was a cheap chowdown at an Italian restaurant.

> Spaghetti marinara
> Garlic bread
> Ice cream
> Bottle of inexpensive Chianti
> White and red–checked tablecloth
> Soft Italian music playing in the background

● Kick up your couple chemistry by shopping for, preparing, and cleaning up the meal together (roll up your sleeves, fill the sink with sudsy water, and indulge in some finger foreplay as you scrub). Take your time and build your sexual appetite. Foreplay doesn't happen only in the bedroom thirty minutes before intercourse. Flirt with each other until you can't wait to devour each other.

● Head to a mattress store and test-drive the beds.

- Take a camera with you on your date. Keep on asking people to take your photo and make it a point to lock lips every time the camera clicks. On your next date, after getting the pictures developed, make a collage of your smooching day.

- Turn your backyard or porch into a home spa for under $25: Pick up a plastic kiddy pool and fill it with water and bubble bath. Pack every safe and available surface with tea lights and turn out the lights. Burn essential oil in a purpose-made burner or light some incense (citrus cents are high on sizzle while keeping mosquitoes at bay). Play some soft background music. When you get out of the "Jacuzzi," wrap yourselves in towels warmed in the dryer. Then massage each other into a delightful daze with lavender-scented lotion (drugstore brands are around $5).

- Skip sex in the tub (the water can cause an infection and your movements will cause a tidal wave on the floor); shampoo each other instead.

  The scalp is an unexplored erogenous zone. Work him into a lather by drizzling a generous helping of shampoo all over his hair. Use slow, small circular strokes and slide down the back of his head, back up toward the top, and all the way to his forehead to make a supersudsy froth. Have a pitcher of clean, warm water handy. Gently tilt his head back, then rinse out the shampoo and wrap his head in a soft towel. Then hand him the shampoo so he can return the favor.

PICKUP DATES

No plan? No problem. Here are four last-minute dates, no forethought required.

1 If you live near a scenic view, turn it into a background location for a make-out sesson at sunset or in the moonlight when the light is romance-perfect for enhancing your sensuous mood.

2 Head to your local department store and challenge each other to come up with the most romantic intimate gift possible for each other. Two things: It can't cost more than $20, and it must be used that night. You'll find that you will really need to think about the essence of each other to come up with an offering that hits the right note. "Frank knows that I love bath products but that I never buy them because they seem too much of a luxury," says Pamela, 38. "So every once in a while, when we're out for the night, he'll pull me into a store and pick out some bath salts or oils. Then, when we get home, he'll run the bath for me, wash me from head to toe and dry me off."

3 Take a walk or drive and use the time to share a naughty fantasy. It's easier to bare your soul about your carnal desires when you aren't face to face. And these conversations are continually necessary since what you want sexually also shifts over time. Cluing each other in on your deepest desires helps to keep your lovemaking fresh and satisfying. Another way to ease into this risqué conversation is to suggest visiting an erotica store. (If you don't have one nearby, wander down the personal massage aisle at your drugstore.)

4 Cruise the aisles of your supermarket and load your cart with whatever epicurean delights you can find: lobster salad, good-quality chocolate, wine or fizzy grape juice, gourmet crackers, gooey cheeses, and so on. Don't forget to get plates, cutlery, and glasses. Now head for the most romantic spot in town and have an impromptu plush picnic. If it's too cold or wet to eat *al fresco,* check to see if there is an atrium at the local zoo, botanical gardens, museum, or mall.

DATING DILEMMAS

You, your partner, a romantic setting, and a chance to kick your couple's chemistry up a notch . . . what could go wrong? Plenty. Here's how to keep your road to love smooth.

Dilemma #1:

You went for a romantic five-courser, and now you feel like an overstuffed pig.

Overloading on a rich repast can make you feel sleepy and fat and not at all sexy. Next time, try sharing a few dishes. It will keep the menu and you feeling lite.

Dilemma #2:

Candlelit dinners and seductive music make you feel like a character in a Harlequin novel— and not in a good way.

Then do what feels sexy to you. Everyone has his or hers own idea of romance. For some, it's a table for two at a four-star restaurant; for others, it's spending the day hiking up a mountain and enjoying the dramatic scenery.

Dilemma #3:

Instead of a night of making mad passionate love, you conked out the minute you got home.

It happens. Don't write off the entire evening. While there's a lot to be said for a bed-bouncing romp, it's the intimate verbal and mental connection you establish when you make time for each other that have the greatest impact on enduring love. Next time, don't wait until you are in your bedroom before heating things up. Start the fire burning with little caresses from the moment you start getting ready for your date. Another tip: Cut your evening short to allow enough time for some horizontal bonding before you get sleepy-eyed once you get home.

Dilemma #4:

You were out for an entire evening and never kissed or cuddled.

These little dating rituals are a way of keeping that loving feeling alive. Think of them as good love habits to keep you in a sizzling frame of mind.

- Make a weekly sofa date. Pick a time and agree to meet at the couch for five minutes, no matter what you are doing at the time. Use those 300 seconds as a life time-out to smooch, hug, say "I love you," or simply gaze into each other's eyes.

- Kick off the weekend by taking a quick stroll in your backyard every Friday night to look at the stars, no matter what the weather.

- Sit down every Saturday morning and have a special breakfast that you both help make. One of you brews the coffee, gets the juice, and sets the table while the other cooks. No newspapers are allowed at the table and no television. Take as much time as you can relishing this quiet time together. (Get up twenty minutes earlier than the kids if this is the only way to make this happen.)

- Celebrate the day of the week that you first started dating by designating that night your time together. Then make it special: Treat each other to a candlelit dinner, rent a movie you saw when you first started dating, or canoodle on the couch.

Chapter 4

DATING . . .
WITH CHILDREN

When you have kids, it's easy to make excuses for not being able to find some dating time for yourselves: The realities of feeding, clothing, and entertaining a family leave little money and energy for nights out on the town. It feels like a full-time job trying to find a good sitter who is actually available when you want to go out. Even if you do manage to get someone, it feels like you barely have the time to take a shower, let alone transform yourself into a dating diva.

No small wonder, then, that it may seem tempting to take your eye off of the relationship ball until your junior set are walking and talking/teenagers/off to college/doing their own sashay down the aisle, but don't. Get out there and flaunt your love.

We think good parenting is about taking care of our children and keeping them safe. But it's also about being their role model. What we forget is that children are sponges, constantly absorbing the world around them. They observe your priorities and what makes you tick. So their ideas about what a strong marriage is and how to eventually form and manage their own relationships come directly from the horse's mouth, i.e., mom and dad and how they relate to each other.

One of the most important love lessons you can give your children is the knowledge that their parents absolutely adore one another and want to spend time together. They need to see love in action. Seems enough incentive to start speed-dialing a sitter right now, wouldn't you say?

REAL-STEAL DEALS

Okay, it's all very well to say call a sitter and get out of there, but what if a sitter is not an option? Maybe you don't have the ducats or a regular sitter. Where there's a will, there's a way. Here are some inexpensive new places to safely park the kids so you and your sweetie can go cruising:

- Call your local Y or recreational center. Most offer programs for children on Friday nights. Call ahead in case you have to reserve a space. Your place of worship may also host a regular Parents Night Out program. "It's a beautiful thing," says Josie, 36, who drops her two children, ages 4 and 7, off at her YMCA on Friday nights. "Four hours for them to play and four hours for us to spend time together. Most of the time we head over to our favorite sushi restaurant and have a great evening talking without worrying about being interrupted by spills, food fights, and crying."

- Check with your local Scout troop to see if they are looking for service projects to fulfill the goals in the achievement program; sitting may fall under that category.

- Make use of grandparents, older neighbors whose grandchildren don't live nearby, or friends who are going through empty-nest syndrome. Or, if you have older kids, put them to work watching the younger ones. Tabitha, 34, says she often hears comments like "How are you able to get out together so much with all those kids?" (She has four, ranging in age from a 1-year-old girl to a 13-year-old boy). "We always involved the older kids in the care of the younger ones so we know that they know how to look after them and don't worry about leaving our son alone with them for a few hours. Plus we don't have to pay them!"

- During school vacations, sign kids up for camp or all-day activities (many classes also take place in the evening).

PICKUP DATES

No plan? No problem. Here are four last-minute dates, no forethought required.

1 Some supermarkets and department stores offer sitting for a few hours while you shop. Sign up your kids and head for the store's café to grab some precious nosh-and-chat time together.

2 If your kids are old enough not to require constant supervision but not old enough to be left on their own in the house, establish monthly overnight camp-outs. Stock up on kid-friendly books (you can get audiobooks if your kids are too young to read), videos, and games; pack a cooler with their favorite drinks and snacks; and set out cereal, bowls, and utensils in the living room. Then tell your kids to get their sleeping bags for a living-room camping trip. They can sleep out in the living room watching videos and playing games and then make their own breakfast in the morning. You and your hubby disappear to another part of the house and make your own fun. (See Chapter 5 for ideas on how to make the best use of your time.) Samantha, 34, loves these at-home-but-separate dates. "My kids are 2, 7, and 11, so it works for all ages. The older kids know how to change the baby's diapers, and we make sure that there are enough different things on hand because of their different ages," she says. "They rarely need us for anything and love being on their own. Best of all, we don't have to pay for a sitter or spend two hours driving to Gran's house twice."

This date works best if you update what your kids are watching or doing so they don't get bored. But with over six hundred new games and movies being released yearly, it can be tough to stay on top of what your kids will find sufficiently entertaining to occupy them for a few hours and you will be happy to have them involved in for several hours. (You can log on to the reviews at edutainingkids.com and commonsensemedia.org to find age-appropriate, parent-approved movies, games, and software.)

While it's unlikely that your kids will stumble across inappropriate violence or sex while duking it out over a board game, the following games (available from boardgames. com, face2facegames.com, and funagain.com) will keep even the youngest glued to their seats without getting bored, frustrated, or needing to have the rules explained yet again.

- For the 3-and-older set try games that don't rely on reading ability. Despite being targeted toward younger players, Knuckling Knights, Zingo, City scape, and Kinder Bunnies: Their First Adventure all have the added advantage of appealing to older kids, too.

- For the 7-and-older set, the competition level can be raised. Try games that rely on think-ahead strategizing like Wildfire, Da Vinci's Challenge, Rumis, and BuyWord.

- For the 10-and-older set, opt for absorbing games that have expansion versions to keep things new and interesting while allowing players of other ages in on the action, such as the Catan series, or cooperative games that require them to work together, like Terra. For more competitive games, Elfenland or Reiner Knizia's Poison require them to constantly make choices that affect the outcome of the game.

3 Choose an activity that is geared totally to kids, such as bowling, miniature golf, skating, mall cruising, or a batting range. If it is something your kids really enjoy doing, you are going to hear less *"euwww"* and "gross" comments as you two kiss and cuddle. Plus their attention will be elsewhere, which means they're less likely to interrupt your conversation.

4 Call all your equally harassed friends with kids and plan a big group picnic with the understanding that you will each be slipping off at some time during the day for some couple's time (if there are a few of you, make up a schedule). If you're really bold, make it a group camping date and stick all the kids in one tent once you've sounded taps.

TEN MUST-DO FAMILY PLAY DATES

While bringing the kids along on your date isn't the ideal solution each and every time you date, the odd the-gang's-all-here expedition can still help strengthen your bond. The key is to think of your "mini–mes" as tag-alongs rather than your official leisure directors, so that the activity you choose is something the adults enjoy as much as—if not more than—the kids. In that

**context, here are ten all-purpose family-style outings
that won't cramp your romantic style:**

1 Your local amusement park. A roller-coaster ride can jolt
you into a save-me! love clinch; a trip through the haunted
house affords ample opportunity to sneak in some grabs or
even a little necking; a challenge to a game of Shoot the Duck
(whoever nabs the teddy bear wins); or a communal stick of
cotton candy (you can slip in a few sugary kisses as you nibble). Some parks offer concerts during the high season, so you
can get down and dance the night—or at least the early
evening—away. To get the scoop on a park near you, check
out themeparkinsider.com/reviews.

2 Check out your local music megastore. Pick up the latest
hot dance CD (if your kids are hip to musical trends, ask them
to help you choose) and plan to make your own after-hours
house party later that evening.

3 See if there is a drive-in movie theater near your home
(driveinmovie.com lists theaters nationwide). Have everyone
wear their PJs and bring a couple of sleeping bags or blankets.
The kids can cozy up in the front seat and watch the show
while you two cuddle in the back.

4 Go rock climbing at an indoor climbing gym. Book the
kids into their own class while you and your honey belay each
other. You don't have to be in great shape (if you can walk up
stairs, you can climb). It's sexy because you need to work as a
team, which means you'll strengthen your union as you scale
the heights.

5 Since being on vacation automatically puts you in a romantic mood, pretend you're from out of town. Most of us take for granted the touristy places in our own backyard, thinking we can visit them any old time, except any old time never rolls around. The chamber of commerce, AAA, or the state or local tourist board will have brochures, maps, guides, and ideas about where to visit. Most areas will have at least some of the following attractions:

- Aquarium
- Zoo
- A site unique to your locale (the birthplace of a famous rock star, the place where a rainbow is mysteriously sighted every year. . .)
- Tours of local industries or factories (just call and ask if you can visit)
- Historical site
- Botanical garden
- Art museum
- Museum of natural history and/or science
- Planetarium or observatory
- Theme and/or amusement park
- Water garden
- Walking tours (guided tours through a city)

Bring the camera and take lots of snaps (get the kids to snap you and your hubby snuggling up in front of famous landmarks), eat at the local hot spot, and, if you can swing it, stay at a nearby hotel (see if they have off-season family rates).

6 Plan for a long, long dinner at an eater-tainment restaurant like Chuck E Cheese, Dave & Busters, Peter Piper Pizza, or Mr. Gatti's. These facilities offer reasonably priced food along with play centers filled with arcade games, kids' rides, pocket billiards, virtual reality and interactive games, table shuffleboard, and a few dozen other attractions guaranteed to keep your younger set (and possibly you) occupied for hours.

7 Instead of planning an activity at a kid-friendly venue with a gang of other similarly sitter-challenged parents, center it around what you love to do. Studies show that one ingredient of a gold-standard relationship is sharing a couple of hobbies. Those benefits also trickle down to the state of your family union. So ignore your kids' groans and gags and follow your passion, whether it's mountain biking or going to ethnic dance shows.

8 Get connected with the thrill of a treasure hunt. Geocaching is a world-wide scavenger hunt where people hide small containers of trinkets in everyday places (buildings, parks, any place you can think of). Your mission is to use a GPS to find them, sign the log, and, if you wish, leave behind a trinket (anything from a film canister to a rabbit's foot). To get clues to a cache near you, log on to geocaching.com, type in your zip code, and go.

9 Let the kids plan the date. Sometimes you can get so stuck in how you do things and thinking with your parenting hat that it can be hard to think of something new, interesting, and fun to do together. Give the children a budget (*aha,* the moment can double-duty as a built-in money-management lesson) and two hours of the day (this way each child gets a turn to have a say in what you do).

10 Go on a bike ride, but rent a tandem for yourselves.

DATING DILEMMAS
....

Dilemma #1:
You can't find a sitter for love or money.

Wouldn't it be nice if all you needed to do was throw a letter up to the clouds, and, *whoosh,* in comes Mary Poppins? Word of mouth is always the best method of finding a sitter. Only problem is, if other parents have someone reliable, they may not be all that eager to blab any details in case you poach their sitter (making her unavailable when *they* need her).

What you need is your own personal on-call child minder. But you may not want to advertise in the local paper or Craig's List in case who-knows-what applies. Try these fresh sources to find someone worthy of watching your precious pumpkins:

- Call your local preschool and see if any teachers or aides are willing to sit in their off hours.
- Check in with your local senior center. Sometimes retired citizens are looking for part-time work.
- Post a notice at the neighborhood teen club or community center.

- If you know someone who has a regular sitter whom they are happy with, see if the sitter has a sibling you can "groom."

- Often schools have newsletters or bulletin boards where jobs can be posted. Some have student placement services that match students up with potential employers.

- Colleges that specialize in early childhood education are a particularly good place to find students genuinely interested in the tender care of your progeny. As a special bonus they may have some background in child development.

- If your child's school or day care has a newsletter, you may be able to place an advertisement.

- Log on to sittercafe.com/index.asp. You "meet" prospective sitters through their online profiles for an annual subscription fee.

- Ask the youth group at your place of worship if they know of congregants interested in sitting. "With five children, date nights are few and far between," says Ray, 35. "When we do get to go out it is because we have had an offer for babysitting from an unsuspecting young person at our church—whom we usually never hear from again!"

- See if there are any au pairs or nannies working in your neighborhood who are available for occasional freelance work (you should check with their employer first).

- Swap leads with your mommy or daddy group.

- If possible, don't make "date night" a Friday or Saturday since those days clash with recreation times for other people, limiting the pool of babysitters. See Chapter 6 for ideas for midweek dates.

Dilemma #2:
Your sitter bagged out at the last minute.

For now, fall back on a last-minute date or arrange a sleepover at a friend or relative's house (make sure you offer to return the favor). So there is no next time, try one of these alternative ideas to hiring a sitter:

- Establish a "Child-care Co-op" with a group of nearby friends and neighbors. A good number to start with is around eight families. Each couple within the group gets an equal amount of coupons. (You can use raffle tickets, poker chips, or playing cards.) Decide on the coupon's value. (A good rule of thumb is each coupon is worth one half-hour of baby-sitting per child.) Get together to lay out the ground rules: bed times, approved TV shows, snacks, and so on, as well as how much advance notice is needed for sitting, what is the penalty if someone is regularly late picking up his or her children, what if you have coupons left over at the end of the month or you need more coupons before the month is up, how to invite a family into the group, when/whether a family may be disqualified, etc. It's good to have everything written down and photocopied so that everyone involved will have a handy reference sheet at home. List contact phone numbers and addresses on the paper as well.

- Swap sitting duties with a couple whom you trust so that you each get one date night per month. It works better if the kids get along well and are close in age so interests and bedtimes don't clash. "My son is fussy about going to sleep with sitters," says Lisa, 43, mother of 5-year-old Will. "So we organized a once-a-month swap with friends where we take turns watching each others' children for a few hours during the day, and then we all have dinner together."

- Use the old bartering system of trading one service for another. Perhaps you know a trusted neighbor or relative who wouldn't mind caring for your children in exchange for a home-cooked dinner (just make twice as much as you would normally) or a washed car.

Dilemma #3:
One of the kids is sick.

There's not much you can do about this. Kids get sick all the time. Take a rain check (and reorganize your sitting options right away so it actually it happens). If the patient sleeps, you might want to try an at-home date (flip over to the next chapter for ideas on what to do).

Chapter 5

STay-aT-HoMe Lovers

ll "date night" really means is intimate, uninter-
rupted, sacred time with the one you love. It doesn't
mean that you have to drop a bundle of cash or
micromanage a deluxe pull-out-the-stops night out or,
for that matter, leave the house at all. However, flop-
ping on the couch, remote in hand, for a night of channel surfing doesn't count. Nor does doing chores, even
if you're doing them together (yes, folding an extra-
large sheet together can turn into an erotic dance of
stolen kisses and caresses between folds, but save it for
another night when romance is not the main event).

You want to make this night special, different from
every other night of the week. The idea is to concentrate
on arranging an evening of togetherness. And since you

feel more at ease in the comfort of your own home, you may be inclined to take risks like eating dinner in the nude or watching an, *ahem,* instructional sex movie.

Never say never; you just don't know where an evening of rubbing up against each other on the sofa might lead . . . as Jessica, 25, discovered. "We came across Laura Corn's *101 Nights of Grrreat Sex: Secret Sealed Seductions for Fun-Loving Couples,* which has lured us to spend most of what would have been our date time indoors! The book has sealed suggestions that we take turns doing to and for each other every week. They are fun and sexy and challenge us to do things we would never have had the courage to just suggest on our own, like role playing. And it gets us in a sexy mood just knowing that we're going to be doing something different."

Read on for everything you need to create a romantic rendezvous while staying in for the evening.

TEN MUST-DO DATES FOR TUCKING IN AT HOME

Get ready to celebrate your one-of-a-kind bond with these amorous adventures without ever leaving the house (or, in some cases, your bed) even once.

1 Transform your home into a five-star resort with these smooth moves:

- Order dinner from a special restaurant and enlist (read "bribe") a friend to act as waiter (promise lunch at a restaurant of choice if he or she will dress the part in fancy duds). Cover a small table-just-for-two with a white cloth and add a candle and a small vase holding just one or two buds. Turn down the lighting, play some soft music, and don't forget to tip your waiter.

- For a total hands-on experience, splurge and book a masseuse to come to your home for a personal rubdown. Expect to pay from $50/hour to untie your knots. (Check with The American Massage Therapy Association, 500 Davis Street, Suite 900, Evanston, IL 60201-4695; toll-free phone: 1-877-905-2700, e-mail: *info@amtamassage.org,* for a reputable therapist in your area.)

- Enough of taking care of everyone else. Put together a sexy spa kit and suggest that you spend your date in the bathroom. (Think of it as couple's therapy.) A steaming hot bath, a candlelit bathroom, plenty of bubbles and scented bath oil, and a big bath sponge will renew your bodies and spirits and keep you enchanted with each other for hours. Throw in a couple of Red Rose Royales (pour an inch of cassis-type liqueur into a flute, add Champagne, and top with a rose petal) to toast your love. When you're done, take turns rubbing each other dry with extra-large bath towels.

• S p i c e   I t   U p •

Removable shower heads can double up as a spicy bath toy.

2 Play Let's Pretend. Getting lost in your own make-believe world can be a sweet, safe way to explore your sexual desires. Act out a naughty fantasy: His stove won't heat and you're the repairwoman; you're Catwoman and he's your Batman. Order costumes from a Halloween catalogue or, if you want to be even more risqué, a sexy costume shop (abcunderwear.com has plenty of racy outfits for men and women—Chippendale dancer, anyone?). Get as outrageous as you like; after all, who is going to see you? (If you have little spinoffs running around, you may want to avoid future therapy bills by parking them at a relative's for the night.)

3 Dim the lights, snuggle up on the couch, and neck like a couple of sweet sixteen-year-olds. Just nuzzle and nibble without any thought to where things might lead. If you have offspring running around, all the better. After all, half the intensity of those teen gotta-have-it make-out sessions was that your parents were often within earshot and might—gasp!—check in on you at any moment. *Bonus:* Your little ones aren't going to ground you if they discover what you are up to. (However, if things do start getting hot and heavy, you will probably want to move the action into a room with a lock.)

4 Nothing gets you in the mood for love like a jaunt to a faraway land. But you don't need to have a passport to enjoy the pulse-pounding pleasures of taking a voyage together. These dates are sure to tantalize your global erogenous zones.

- Have a luau: Set the scene with leis, grass skirts, and a cardboard palm tree cutout (available from most party supply stores). Unless pork puts you in heat, give the spit-roasted pig a pass. Instead, pick up easy-to-find tropical fruits like mangos, papayas, pineapples, and coconuts from the supermarket to cut into small pieces to feed each other. Mix up a couple of piña coladas topped with hot-pink paper umbrellas. Add a travel video on Hawaii or old *Hawaii 5-0* tapes for background entertainment and a bottle of tropical massage oil for an aloha massage.

• S p i c e I t U p •

Treat him to his own private hula dance.

- Create a night in Paris by turning your living room or kitchen into a little bistro (but skip the Gitane cigarettes). Decorate a card table with an old wine bottle as a candleholder, play an Edith Piaf CD, write up your menu on a large chalkboard and prop it up, and, if you don't have dark lamp shades, use red bulbs to create a sexy glow. Serve up steak frites and a bottle of rouge and speak to each other in silly French accents. *Ooh-la-la!*

- Instead of having dinner at that Italian place that you always go to, create your own table for two at a garden restaurant in Florence. Plan to eat no earlier than ten P.M. Dress up your backyard picnic table with a red and white–checkered tablecloth and a couple of tall, tapered white candles. Play opera music in the background. Add in pasta florentine with a bottle of Chianti, and biscotti and a couple of blood oranges for dessert, and you'll be making out like Latin lovers before the night is done. That's amore!

- Plan a night of Eastern pampering. Clear the furniture off of the rug and stack the space high with comfy cushions to lounge on during your meal. Add a bowl of water filled with blossoms such as white lilies and light some jasmine incense. Pick up some Asian take-out and a bottle of plum wine or sake.

• S p i c e I t U p •

For dessert order some raunchy fortune cookies, often available from sex shops (google "X-rated fortune cookies" for suppliers).

5 Meet for a midnight snack. Nibble on whatever sweet thing is on hand or have a s'mores tent party. Hook up a makeshift tent with a rope and a blanket, then roast a couple of marshmallows in the toaster oven and sandwich them with chocolate graham crackers. Don't worry about making yourself a sticky mess; you can lick the crumbs off of each other later.

6 Even if you're not handy, you can still work on a home project together. But skip the kitchen paint job, no matter how necessary, and work on something that can be used for future home dates, like converting your shower to a steam unit or building a gazebo hideaway in the garden for lover's trysts. Working together to improve your home reminds you of the commitment you made to share a life together. To get the job done, you'll need teamwork and communication. (We promise that the satisfaction that comes with creating something together will long outlast the memory of him accidentally hitting your big toe with the hammer.) Chances are a few screwups will be made along the way, so be prepared to laugh instead of yell. The Web site kitguy.com will tool you up for everything from constructing porch swings to in-house saunas.

7 Get cooking together and create a sexy feast just for two.

- If you love good eating but hate the thought of preparing anything more complicated than boil-in-a-bag rice, then order up a prepared gourmet meal that can be easily served at home. You can have almost anything delivered such as lobsters (including shell crackers and seafood forks, bibs and moist towelettes, fresh whole lemon and butter, and a cooking manual starting at $59.95, from livelob.com) or a three-course international spread (at gourmetstation.com, you can get a Parisian, Tuscan, Cajun, or fusion appetizer, main meal, and dessert delivered anywhere, starting at $69.99).

- Pick up a cooking magazine and choose a recipe more complicated than you would usually make and then prepare it together. (Do like the top chefs and keep a couple of glasses of wine on hand to sip from between sautés.)

- Have a pizza night and make your own customized pies (heart-shaped, of course). You can pick up premade dough at most supermarkets or improvise with English muffins or pita bread as your base.

- Try to re-create your favorite restaurant meal.

8 "A jug of wine, a loaf of bread, and thou . . ." You don't have to wait for a nice sunny day to share a romantic meal al fresco. When you take the action indoors, you can picnic any time. Spread a green tarp in the living room for "grass." Drag in some plant pots to add some greenery. Turn a fan on low to create a warm spring breeze. Keep the picnic basket simple: Use paper and plastic and easy to prepare cold-serve food. A loaf of French bread, a couple different cheeses, a container of Greek olives, roast chicken, fresh melon and strawberries for dessert, and something to drink is the perfect picnic repast. Best of all, you won't have to worry about ants.

9 Make a mixed tape or CD together. Pick a theme such as Tunes to Make Love To, Our Love Story in Music, Our Greatest Hits, or Our Favorite Dirty Dances. Or re-create your high school dream of forming your own band. At createbands.com, you'll be able to create a rock band and hear it play music online. Then find a van to shake, rock, and roll in.

10 Fire up your sex life by checking out the latest how-to sex-advice books. *The Joy of Sex* (Crown, 2002) by Alex Comfort, *Position of the Day: Sex Every Day in Every Way* by Lorelei Sharkey and Emma Taylor (Chronicle Books, 2003) and *The Bedside Orgasm Book: 365 Days of Sexual Ecstasy* (Fairwinds Press, 2005) by Cynthia Gentry are all tomes that have easy-to-put-into-practice ideas for passionate study.

• Spice It Up •

If you're more of a visual learner, try these sexy technique videos: *New Sex Now: Life's Ultimate Pleasure* (New Sex Institute, 2003), *Kama Sutra: Sensual Art—Positions* (Full Circle, 2002), and *Loving Sex—Erotic Strip Dance—Capture His Passion* DVD & CD set (Alexander Institute, 2004) are all sure to get two thumbs-up (and possibly more) from both of you.

SEXTREME MAKEOVERS

The best things in life aren't free; they're easy. Here, simple touches for your home that are sure to kick the romantic heat up a notch or three.

• House of Love •

There is an art to romancing at home, and it doesn't include the latest masterpiece by your mini Picasso spread out on the kitchen table, piles of unfolded laundry on the couch, or rubber duckies in the bathtub

(unless they're the kind with built-in vibrators: google "ducky vibrator" if you want one of those!). Here's your step-by-step guide to romantic home improvements you can make in five minutes or less (no candles included).

1 Put away all electronic devices (no phone, computer, or TV unless it's a planned part of your date—you're watching a video or burning a CD). If you have bambinos on board, by all means keep the baby monitor on, but put it out of the way so it isn't taking its usual center stage (that means taking it off of its triple-knotted necklace and putting it on a shelf in whatever room you are in). The fine for disobeying this rule is one sexual favor.

2 Put the cat out for the night and any other inquisitive animal. If the animals are your kids, make sure there is a lock on the bedroom door.

3 Clean up all the clutter. You don't have to make things spic and span; shove everything in the closet if you need to, but get it out of your line of vision (and thoughts).

4 Lower the room temperature; you'll feel more inclined to cuddle and snuggle together (as if you need any extra incentive).

5 Ignite a fire or, if you don't have a hearth, light several candles around the room for the same effect; just remember to blow them out before you create your own inferno. Or tack up strands of Christmas lights for a magical glow.

• Spice It Up •

Using fabric glue, stick glow-in-the-dark stars onto a black sheet. When the glue has dried, hang the sheet up so that it resembles a tent. Arrange pillows and blankets inside for a romantic night under the stars.

6 Perfume the room, but skip the incense and put out a bowl of lavender-scented soaps or Good 'n' Plenty instead. It's a fact: Both of these surprising scents have the power to work you and your huggy bear into a suggestive state.

• How to Pick Lingerie That You Both Love, Love, Love •

Don't forget to give yourself a foxy update.

Not just for him (although he will much appreciate the effort and hopefully catch the hint that he needs to pay attention to his own bedtime wardrobe). It feels good to get in touch with your girly-girl side. Even if it makes you feel silly to prance around in bits of silk at first, so what? Who said getting sexy had to be serious stuff? What keeps the carnal dance constantly interesting is stepping outside of the way you usually do things and injecting some variety in your love twirls. So go ahead and slip into that lacy little number (you probably have half a dozen shoved in the back of your drawer waiting for that special night that never seems to be tonight). The most pulse-pumping colors are black, purple, or red. Various shades of beige, tan, or brown are also hot winners because they look like skin tone, so you seem naked. If you're not gaga for garters and stilettos, choose a teddy or nightgown that barely covers your derrière instead.

EMERGENCY ROMANCE RATIONS

It's eight P.M. You're both home and awake. Any kids in the house are actually out (asleep or truly off-premises) for the night. None of your favorite TV shows are on. Although as rare as an ivory-billed woodpecker, these moments do happen. What to do?

Make like a scout and always be prepared by keeping these books, music, and games on hand for those times when you want to throw together a spur-of-the-moment at-home date (check out Chapter 1 for movie title suggestions).

• Five Must-Have Books •

From sexy to gushing, these titles may have you bookmarking the pages and creating some of your own action:

1. A love coupon collection such as *Steamy Coupons* or *Hot Sex Coupons* from Sourcebooks (or make your own personalized version using a raffle ticket book).

2. *52 Saturday Nights: Heat Up Your Sex Life Even More with a Year of Creative Lovemaking* (Warner Books, 2000) by Joan Elizabeth Lloyd: A week-by-week course in pleasure.

3. *The 50 Greatest Love Letters of All Time* (Crown, 2002) by David Lowenherz: As this book reveals, there are an infinite number of ways to say "I love you."

4. *Sensual Massage for Couples* (Arcata Arts, 2001) by Gordon Inkeles: Learn the massage techniques that will make your mate beg for more.

5. *Love: Ten Poems* (Miramax Books, 1995) by Pablo Neruda: In Spanish with English translations, you can take turns reading this romantic short collection of sensual sonnets out loud to each other.

•Eight Must-Have Good Lovin' Albums•

These CDs will get you moving and grooving to a romantic beat.

1. & 2. SOUL/FUNK: If Stevie Wonder's *Songs in the Key of Life* or James Brown's *20 All-Time Greatest Hits* don't make you want to get out of your chair and shake your booty, then someone ought to check your pulse.

3. & 4. COUNTRY: *Essential Tammy Wynette* and George Jones's *She Thinks I Still Care* will take you through their tumultuous love story (and make you grateful for your own tamer tale).

5. JAZZ: *The Essential Miles Davis* is as cool and smooth as it gets.

6. NEW AGE: *Numinous* by Skaroulis is uplifting and melodic without the usual synthetic elevator rhythm that so much of this style is prone to.

7. R&B: *Al Green—Greatest Hits* has some of the sexiest, most soulful love songs of all time.

8. CLASSIC LOVE SONGS: Frank Sinatra can be counted on to swoon anyone into the mood. Try his *Songs for Swingin' Lovers,* and you'll soon be making whoopee.

• Six Must-Have Games •

Playing games is about to get a whole lot sexier.

- Scrabble (Milton Bradley). Pulling out a seven-letter, triple-word score with a "Q" is pretty damn sexy. Give plus or minus points for using romantically themed vocabulary (have a *Webster's* on hand in case things get messy).

- DaVinci's Challenge (Briarpatch): This MENSA select award-winning game will have you pitting smarts. Winner gets to choose how you end the evening.

- Clue (Parker Brothers): This game is tailor-made for making up some titillating fantasies: Mr. Green and Mrs. Peacock getting it on in the drawing room. Add to the fun and dress your part.

- Have a "Strip PlayStation" Challenge: What's more fun than cleaving your partner's head off with a laser scimitar? Every time a character is killed, you must remove a piece of clothing. For hot gaming action that doesn't make you feel like an extra in *Girls Gone Wild,* try something from the Stolen series for PS2, where you get to play a sexy, smart, female thief and he can choose from a variety of studlike characters.

- Do a jigsaw puzzle together. There is something to be said about enjoying comfortable silences as you work as a team to fit the pieces together. Try a 3-D puzzle and build entire cities. Or use a blank puzzle (available from craft stores) to create your own picture or love message.

- If it's a wild night of lovin' you're after, the Kama Sutra Game (Relationship Enrichment Systems) will turn your date night upside down, backward, and every which way.

PICKUP DATES

No plan? No problem. Here are four last-minute dates, no forethought required.

1 The kids are at soccer practice? Use the hour to have a breakfast-in-bed date. You can whip up this romantic meal in less than fifteen minutes: Cut toasted bread into pretty shapes and serve with fruit jam and butter, fresh-brewed coffee and cream, linen napkins, and bud vase with a flower. (You can make a craft flower by twisting a pipecleaner around some crumpled colored tissue paper or Kleenex if you don't have any flowers on hand.)

2 Write a love poem together. You don't have to be budding Shakespeares or even be able to rhyme to put together a few mushy phrases. Just write from the heart. (If you need inspiration, start with, "I love you more . . . ")

3 Try this kissing challenge: One hundred kisses in one hour (or however much time you have). Make it even more blissful with these mouth-to-mouth moves:

- Rub your bodies together as your lips touch to keep the sexual connection cranked up high.

- Vary between light feathery kisses and deep tongue teasers.

- Don't limit yourself to the lips; smooch and smack each other from head to toe.

4 Curl up together with the paper's Suduko challenge. Sharing smarts is foreplay with a brain. You can add to the sexual tension with a little seduction by the numbers: Make your back #1, breasts #2, his bottom #3, and so on. Whenever you figure out a number in the puzzle, you caress the corresponding body part. Try REDBOOK'S *Sudoku: Grids to Go* (Hearst Books, 2007).

REAL-STEAL DEALS

By its very nature, staying at home is cheap: It usually involves no sitter, no dinner bill, no tip, and no gas. These are great get-together moments that cost nothing at all.

- Challenge him to a sexy Olympics. Good-bye to the boredom of track and field, and hello to the sport of bed and sofa. There could be games in which length, duration, style, ingenuity, and endurance all play a part. Try customizing events to your own sexual imagination. The cross-country run can be adapted to the cross-yard tryst (handicaps can be introduced in the form of garden furniture, interfering neighbors, pets, and kiddy toys). The one-hundred meters can be a team activity, in which you see how fast you can race toward a sexual finish line. (The gold is automatically given for reaching it simultaneously.)

- Transform your bedroom into a getaway retreat by setting it up as a hotel room, complete with number on the door, mints on a freshly made bed (use crisp white cotton sheets), a huge stack of towels and a few fizzy bath tablets in the bathroom (for an instant Jacuzzi), nice stationery and a pen (for writing each other love notes), a bottle of something chilling in an ice bucket, and room service.

- Kiss and hug in the dark while watching for the International SpaceStation to make its daily pass. For sighting info, go to heavens-above.com.

- Turn your date into a treasure hunt that has you meeting in the bedroom to collect your prizes (each other). Hide anything you think you will want for your date night—music, food, clothing for each of you to wear—and write your clues (for example, start with a note directing him to the fridge, so he can find the drinks and glasses you stashed there).

- Play strip poker, shedding one item of clothing every time you lose. See if you can make it through more than just a few hands.

Staying at home for your date means it can be harder to get away from it all. Here's how to keep from slipping into a rut:

Dilemma #1:

You want to finish this one last chore.

It's all too tempting when you home-date to just get on with your daily grind. You think that you'll just tidy up a bit before you light the scented candles and maybe you should scrub the scum out of the tub before adding the rose petals and, before you know it, your idyllic interlude has become a night of the same old, same old. Stop the madness. Draw up a new to-do list for setting a romantic atmosphere. Number one is to build anticipation by sending your honey a flirty come-on, inviting him to meet you in your home for a night of intimacy. Call, make a homemade card using an old snap of the two of you, write a love ditty ("I adore thee and want a night home free") or a send an e-vite (*www.evite.com*). Then, at the start of your date, do whatever you need to do to get in a starry-eyed mood, whether it's play a certain sweet song, slip into something silky, or simply start the night with a long, make-you-weak-at-the-knees kiss with your resident loverboy.

Dilemma #2:

The kids woke up and busted up your fun.

It happens. If you can't pick up where you left off, don't kill the entire at-home date idea. Plan a rain check date right away to take place within the next week. This time, keep the kids active during the day to try and conk them out for the entire night. Or banish them for the evening by organizing a sleepover at a friend's (yours or theirs) or relative's house. Or work around them. Carol, 34, and Richard, 35, have three young children running around the house during their home-date nights, so she knows things will rarely go smoothly. "But when it's the only break from wall-to-wall work and parent time we get in the week, we really suffer the loss of our date nights, so we really make the best of it whatever happens. Recently, our 1-year-old wouldn't go to sleep, our 2-year-old wouldn't stop crying, and our 5-year-old wouldn't stop whining. So we ended up having 'date breaks' by hiding in the hall closet, meeting every fifteen minutes for a kiss and cuddle or a bite of dinner. It was probably the most fun we had ever had on a date!"

Dilemma #3:

A pipe breaks and floods your bedroom, the burglar alarm goes off and the police come, the baby won't go to sleep, your neighbor came over to borrow your drill just as you had stripped down for your fresh-air picnic in the nude.

Doesn't it always seem that just when you are planning that special evening, everything that can go wrong will? Don't sweat it. A good marriage is a lively, fun relationship between two people who both get the joke. It's being able to hoot at the unexpected that both defines and bonds you as a couple, which is the whole reason for having a date night in the first place. As Alysson, 28, says, "Once our son came along and date night became home-date night and usually interrupted date night, my husband and I realized it didn't really matter what we did on our dates as long as we had a chance to talk and laugh together."

Dilemma #4:
You're not in the mood, or he isn't.

In your mind, date night—and especially at-home date night—and sex may go together like love and marriage, in that you can't do one without the other, except . . . the libido is a fickle, ephemeral thing. Expecting it to perk up just because you have managed to work in some couple time is like assuming that you'll have a sock-rolling orgasm every time you make love. It would be nice, but is it a sure thing? Absolutely not. Just check out the conditions your libido is having to work under: The average date lasts less than four hours and usually comes at the end of a day chockablock with the usual kids-work-house-life stuff. You're both mentally and physically tired and stressed and perhaps not a little cranky. Sexy stuff. No! Try this: Instead of focusing on the end goal of SEX, simply caress and kiss and cuddle for the sheer pleasure of taking a leisurely physical time-out with the one you love. It may be that you tickle your desires awake, or it may be that you fall asleep in each other's arms. So be it. Sweet dreams.

quickie Dates

A t the start of a romance, when you are busy spilling the details of your life, it's hard to imagine a future where you won't want to spend every waking second with each other endlessly talking and confiding in each other. But, as your love becomes more solid, you develop a sort of couple's shorthand that enables you to get your point across without a lot of conversation: You immediately understand that when he makes his meatloaf special for dinner that work was crazed today, and he knows that when you say you went to the bank today that you paid the bills this month, no further discussion required.

Perhaps you think nothing happened in your day that's worth relating in depth. Or maybe you just need to relax during your down time, and part of that is having some quiet time. But couples bond best when they're deeply involved in each other's lives. It's the everyday stories and not the big, momentous, "You'll-never-guess-what-happened-today" sagas that create empathy and intimacy. If you two aren't sharing the details of your time apart, you may feel yourself losing your sense of connection.

It doesn't matter if your day was spent caring for the kids or designing rocket launchers. Your conversation doesn't have to be a ten-page memo. Tales of a difficult boss, your micro version's latest cleverness, a mesmerizing new song heard on the radio, or a fleeting sexy thought you had in the shower—these are the tidbits that bind. Maybe the only memorable thing that happened this week was that you needed to fill the car tires with air. Talking about it may lead to a discussion about hybrid cars, which may meander to a memory of a driving vacation you took last year. The thing is, unless you start talking, you never know where the conversation may end up.

The trick is creating time to unwind and chat when you feel like you don't even have the time to talk to yourself. These speed dates maximize whatever pauses you do have together, even if it's just fifteen minutes during the week, to get you in each other's loop. Be warned: Your Monday–Friday schedule is about to get a lot more interesting!

TEN MUST-DO SPEED-DATES FOR SUPERBUSY COUPLES

Take a breath. If you can't even begin to imagine trying to squeeze some get-close talk time into your already bustling schedules, then these snappy mini dates are tailor-made for you:

1 Cruise by the bakery section of your supermarket and pick up something really sinful for dessert. Then cozy up together on the couch and take turns feeding each other.

2 Choose a night during the workweek and reserve an "I Love You Hour." Use this time to toast yourselves and tell each other at least one specific thing that happened this week that reminded you how lucky you are to have each other. It'll feel a bit forced at first, but once you get in the habit of celebrating your bond, you will find yourself looking for things throughout the week to bring up.

• Spice It Up •

Get inspiration from watching your wedding video. (Focus on the love-you-4-eva moments and gloss over the what-was-I-thinking? bridal party clothes.)

3 Start a weekly ritual of watching a TV show together, but don't just tune in and zonk. Pick something that never in a million years would you normally view. It's okay if the show turns out to be a bomb. Taking yourselves out of your comfort zone can launch unexpected discussions.

4 If exercising is already a part of your weekly routine, make a plan to limber up together. It'll feel less like a chore and more like a we're-in-this-together moment when you help each other to get your hearts pumping and cheer each other along. Besides, it's just plain sexy to work up a sweat together.

• S p i c e I t U p •

Challenge yourselves with something different like kickboxing or hula-hooping.

5 Abbreviate your idea of together time with a mini date. Think a half-hour for a pizza lunch for two or one quick cocktail or coffee together after work. "The important thing is getting time together," agrees Courtney, 28. "There have been times when we squeezed in a quick meal before my husband had to return to work. But spending that hour together was better than not having any time alone with each other that week."

6 Adjust your clocks and have a daytime date. You don't have to wait until the sun sets to have a hot date. Meet during your lunch hour and grab a bite together or drop the kids off for a class at your local museum and go browsing through the exhibits by yourselves.

7 If you both drive to work, put on the Ritz and rent a limo to make that commute home together after work a swanky romantic spree (expect to pay between $50 and $150 per hour). Most cars are equipped with a mini bar, flowers, and gobs of space to get lovey-dovey.

• Spice It Up •

Don't rush your hour. Take an extra cruise around the block.

8 Morning, when you're both bright-eyed and bushy-tailed as opposed to end-of-the-day just plain bushed, is a great time to have a restorative respite together. Plan on having breakfast or, if time is too tight for even a bagelicious moment, a wake-up coffee together once a week at the same local diner. (Once you've been a regular for a while, you won't even have to waste minutes ordering, since they will know to serve you your "usual.") Whether it's a charming café or a truck stop, the fact that you make it your own date place will make it feel special.

9 Meet for some afternoon delight at a no-tell motel. It doesn't have to be a dive (it's hard to feel like a sexy siren when you don't want to put your bare bottom on the sheets). Even some of the swankier hotels rent rooms by the hour for business meetings, so check what's available in your area. Use the time to make buttons fly while you rip off each other's clothes or simply to burrow and whisper sweet nothings. Make sure you pack some candles and music to give the room a ten-second romantic makeover.

• S p i c e   I t   U p •

Because nothing is more fun than being bad together,
slip a bathing suit on under your daily wear and crash
the pool at a local hotel.

10 Instead of gearing up to high speed from the moment you
open your eyes, wake up to an indulgence. Set the alarm to get
up extra early and have breakfast in bed together. It'll bring
back those lazy-dazy Sunday mornings after the Saturday date
night when you had no particular place to go or thing to do
other than savor each other's sweet company.

REAL-STEAL DEALS

**While it's unlikely that grabbing a small block of recess
with your mate is going to break the weekly budget,
these zippy love moments cost absolutely nothing more
than your time.**

● Bask together in the warmth of a new day. Wake him up
early so you can snuggle under a blanket and watch the sun
rise over the horizon together. Use this classic romantic
moment to lean in close as if you are going to whisper something just for him in his ear. Instead, surprise him with this
real little eye opener: Nibble his lobe and softly caress his
skin with your hot breath.

• S p i c e   I t   U p •

After the sun show, you could just go back to sleep.
Or you could return to bed and make your own
sparks.

- Make a weekly date to end the weekend with a late-night arm-in-arm stroll together, even if it's just around your backyard. Get in sync by matching your steps.

• Spice It Up •

Take a heady detour into some dark nook or cranny that you normally zip by and steal a few kisses.

- Multitask clearing out the fridge by packing up all the leftovers for a picnic. Add your best china and glassware, and then make a date to meet at your local park during your lunch hour.

- Give in to the undeniably kitschy romantic allure of standing together and watching the sun go down. Head to the highest point in town so you can see the twinkling lights of the houses below turn on as the sky darkens.

- Make a phone date to talk for fifteen minutes. This is different from hitting the speed dial to remind him that you'll be late tonight or to pick up milk on the way home. Ink it into your calendar and make sure you are in a space where there are no other distractions (screaming kids, nosy coworkers, cheery checkout workers, and so on) so you can give each other your full attention. You can keep your conversation G-rated with clue-ins to how your day is going. But if you want to make a carnal call, here are a few tips to get a ringy-dingy without losing your connection.

   1. Lose the nerves. The best part of making a phone-sex date with your partner is that even if things

don't go as smoothly as planned, you don't have to worry about whether he'll call you in the morning!

2. The main thing is to have an idea of what you are going to say before you dial his digits. Otherwise, you may find yourself speechless when he picks up. You can share your sexy desires, describe the details of your hot love session with him, whisper a steamy fantasy, or murmur what you would love to do to him right now.

3. Also, remember, the best porn movies involve a sexy buildup. So don't feel compelled to start breathing how hot you are right after he says his hellos. Chat for a few minutes about your day and gradually up the erotic ante by telling him that you wish he were with you . . . and then tell him why. Or tell him what you are wearing (pink silk crotchless panties, even if you are wearing the same pair of sweats for the third day running). Or you can let him take the lead and bring the conversation over to the kinky side.

4. If aural sex seems too risky, try a play-date call with two Dixie cups and a piece of string. Or make a date to cyber-romance each other. Instead of using your downtime to play computer solitaire, e-mail each other your love thoughts on a daily basis. You don't need to write a love sonnet; Gina, 33, and her husband Carl, 35, e-mail each other a dozen times a day with quick messages about something funny that just happened or a comment on a conversation they had at breakfast. "It may be no more than a line or two, but it adds up," she says. "By the time we meet up at the end of the day, we don't have to catch each other up because we've been connecting all day." (Warning: Be careful with sending sexy notes to each other at work, as 55 percent of companies review employer e-mails and a quarter have fired workers for e-mail abuse.)

PICKUP DATES

No plan? No problem. Here are four last-minute dates, no forethought required.

1 There is something movie-moment romantic about a blackout, but you don't have to wait for the electric company to malfunction to create your own private lights out. Forbid all use of electricity (yes, that includes the cell phone and computer) and close all the curtains. Light a few candles and then play shadow games on each other's bodies.

2 Conserve water by taking a bath together. If you don't have any bath oils handy, puree a piece of cucumber and pour the juice into the bath water. Yes, it sounds crazy, but, according to research, the scent is a sexual stimulant for men and women. However, if you can't stomach the thought of turning your tub into a salad bowl, stir in a few teaspoons of vanilla extract or lavender seeds.

3 Knead each other. Studies show that all it takes is fifteen minutes of massage to rub those stress hormones right out of your system. Here are three simple-to-master techniques:

- **STROKING THE TEMPLE:** Buddhists believe that the center of the forehead (sometimes called the third eye) is also the center of the soul. Begin by supporting your partner's head in your hands with your fingers at the base of the skull. Massage the entire scalp, gradually working your hands to the temples. Continue pressing upward to the crown of the head. Then press in the middle of the forehead at the hairline with your thumbs. Don't be surprised if he or she sighs, *"Oohm."*

- **NECK MOVES:** For many people, the neck and shoulders are common areas of soreness and tension. Ease the pain with the right stroke. The muscles that run up the neck are thick and respond well to manipulations with the thumbs. The muscles that run downward to the spine are thinner and can be pressed with the heel of the hand.

- **FOOT RUB.** To rev up tired hooves, gently hold his or her foot in one hand and use the other hand to massage the sole of the foot with your thumb. Begin with the area directly below the large toe. After initial pressure, roll the thumb back and forth (use the same wiggly motion you would use in a thumb war). Release the pressure and move on to the area below the next toe, gradually working all five piggies.

4 Hop in the car and cruise through your town's wealthiest neighborhood. But instead of just ogling the palatial homes, talk about what you think the houses might look like on the inside or make up stories about the people who live there.

DATING DILEMMAS

While regular fifteen-minute interludes of togetherness can add up to enough bonding time to keep your relationship on a happy track, it can still be stressful to feel like there is a time limit (however necessary) on your loving moments. Here's how to relax and not feel like you are dating under a buzzer.

Dilemma #1:

You feel like you never have enough time to even think about what you would do on a full-night date.

Make your next date at a fountain and take turns throwing pennies in, making a wish (out loud) about what you would like to do on your next date night. Then do it!

Dilemma #2:

Crunching time in together makes your date feel like one more chore on your to-do list.

Make your fifteen minutes of date time out-of-the-ordinary wonderful. Massage a part of each other's body that normally doesn't get loving attention, write each other love letters or dream lists and then read them to each other, share an ice cream cone and let your tongues fight over the next lick, wait for the first star to come out and make a wish together or simply murmur to each other all the ways that you love each other. "Our lives are crazy," states Tracy, 23. "My soon-to-be husband works rotating shifts of days and nights, and when he is at work he's gone about fifteen hours a day. And I look after our 6-month-old son. To help us reconnect, we started this ritual of hugging as we tell each other what has happened during the time we were apart. Holding each other close helps put us into a close place."

Dilemma #3:

Your weekly date to watch a TV show has turned into a nightly date of vegging out in front of the tube.

Start taking advantage of those commercials (if you use TiVo, stop!). Instead of watching how your toothpaste is a newer and improved version, mute the volume and talk, even if all you end up talking about is how "new and improved" is usually just the same old thing in new, smaller packaging.

• Spice It Up •

Try turning the TV off and reading the newspaper or a magazine to each other instead. Pick an article that you are both likely to be interested in.

Dating off the Beaten Path

When you two were brand new, just going to dinner and a movie together was a thrilling adventure because there was the very good chance that it would yield some yet undiscovered nugget: He likes mustard and ketchup on his cheeseburgers! You won't eat your movie snack until the main feature starts! These little tidbits would gradually build up until you were involved in an info free-for-all, revealing everything from your hopes for the future and your political thoughts to your preferred sexual moves and why you sometimes hate your sister. But eventually, as you grew more solid as a couple, dinner and a movie became just that: A nice, cozy night out with the one you love.

It's not that there is nothing new to know about each other. Unless you are an amoeba, you are always changing, growing, and evolving. But we tend to think of intimacy as a static thing, a goal to be achieved rather than a land to be explored and re-explored throughout your relationship. The result? Yawn.

The good news is that it doesn't take much to re-create that "Who-is-this-fascinating-creature?" feeling. It doesn't even necessarily require a huge amount of time, just an adjustment of consciousness. One of the simplest ways a couple can keep their relationship alive, intriguing, and vibrant, is to throw it a curve by going on a date that is exciting, wacky, adventurous, even a bit scary every once in a while. (Make every date a challenge, and the biggest risk you'll end up running is exhaustion from having to constantly raise the bar.) Daring to be silly and open to the unexpected occasionally can bring out facets of each other's personality that you didn't know existed.

A nice little side effect: Your sex life will also probably be zippier. Desire thrives on the unknown and adores the uninhibited. Bingo! Ready to try these dates that push you out of your comfort zone?

TEN MUST-DO DATES TO TRY BEFORE YOUR NEXT ANNIVERSARY

If money were no object, our poll found that you would overwhelmingly like to do something not just romantic but also wild and crazy. You don't have to wait until you win the lottery to put some hip into your hop. Yes, some of the following think-outside-the-Saturday-night-at-eight box dates might be a bit more than you would normally dole out, but, then again, doesn't your love affair deserve the occasional splurge?

1 Amp up the fear factor. When life is a fairly safe, secure, and controlled affair (you have an idea of what most of the day holds and can pretty much predict that you will not be attacked by flesh-feeding aliens any time soon), it can be a rush to purposely put yourselves in a scary situation, however faux the actual danger may be. According to medical experts, here's what it's like to feel really petrified: a pounding heart-beat, faster breathing, nervous perspiration, butterflies in the stomach. *Hmmm,* that sounds uncannily how that first flush of a new relationship feels, which is why exploring your fear boundaries with your partner and then mastering that fear by working through it together can help cleave your couplehood and elevate you to new bonded heights.

Just playing the trust game, where you fall backward and your partner (hopefully) catches you, may be enough to put you in a cold sweat. Or you may thrive on more heart-in-your-mouth moments on one of the fright nights listed here.

• Dates to Scare Yourselves Silly On (If You Dare) •

- Go bungee jumping.

- Try a parachute jump.

- Take a trapeze class.

- Take a ride on the scream machine at your local amusement park.

- Check out fright night (special scary events usually scheduled around the Halloween season).

- Watch a horror film. According to one study, these are the scariest movies ever made: *The Exorcist* (1973), *Halloween* (1978), *Friday the 13th* (1980), *The Shining* (1980), *Poltergeist* (1982), *Nightmare on Elm Street* (1984), *Scream* (1996).

2 Spend a day at the races or check out the action at a casino. Marriage is all about gambling. Think about the adrenalin high you were on at your wedding, and no wonder; when you exchange vows, you're essentially throwing caution to the wind and betting that you will spend the rest of your life with this person. Making a wager, no matter how small, is one way to recapture that head rush. You don't even have to make a money stake to get the feeling: Play a card game, such as Phase10, and make the winnings a week off from house chores or breakfast in bed.

3 Go to a fortune teller. It doesn't matter if she gets it right. (Do you really need a crystal ball to tell you that you're meant for each other?) But it can be a giggle (if she's wrong) or inspiring (if she's in the ballpark) to hear how a total stranger reads your romance.

4 Break out of your daily mold. If you're an urban babe, try a visit to a farm. A museum is his usual date choice? Suggest a circus instead. Are you veteran line dancers who wouldn't be seen out of your boots on a Saturday night? Sign up for a ballroom-dancing class. Familiarity breeds contempt. You occasionally need an element of surprise and dare to keep things sweet and sexy between you. Even if it ends up being something you swear you'll never do again, the date will go down as a shared "remember when" moment in your relationship history and keep you laughing for years.

5 Make a date to meet at an unusual time such as two in the afternoon or seven in the morning. You'll feel less like a card-carrying long-term couple trying to plan some quality together time and more like a pair of illicit lovers squeezing in a rendezvous behind everyone's back.

6 One of the staples of American romance has been the horse. In the old movies, when the hero got the girl, what did they do? They rode off into the sunset together. If you don't know how to ride or there are no stables in your area, go for a jaunt in a horse-drawn carriage or a whirl on a mechanical horse (wear your tightest jeans). *Yippee-ki-yo-ki-yay!* Or scoot off Italian-lover style on a Vespa rental.

7 It has been a long, hard day/week/year. Your patience is already paper thin, you get into the car, and you see that he didn't refuel after driving to the gym last night. Again.

Meanwhile he's fuming because you forgot to bring the lawn mower in for repairs. The last thing you feel like doing is making nice on your date night. So don't. Take out your irritation while trying to blow each other to smithereens from the cockpits of SIAI Marchetti SF260s. The weapons are simulated, but the airborne dogfight is real. These are not simulated flights. You fly with an experienced pilot, but you get to do the "shooting." Go to aircombatusa.com and find a location near you. But start saving now; it will cost you around $2,000 for the pleasure of blasting each other out of the sky. Or head for a cheaper version and take aim (at the target, not each other) at a rifle or archery range.

8 Knock his socks off by suggesting you check out a strip club together. Yes, really. Many are female-friendly joints these days so you won't feel like you're the only woman with her breasts covered (but try to choose a "gentleman's club," as they tend to be classier than your average strip bar). You'll find that being a player, as opposed to a passive object of lust, is very empowering. Plus, you'll make him very, very happy, not just because of the floor show, or because you might pick up a trick or two to try on him later on that night, but mostly because, as reports from all over (but especially from the men) suggest, right up there with more sex (and more oral sex), the one thing he wants is for you to take the sexual lead more often. Bottom line: He needs to know that you get as much pleasure thinking about sex as you do thinking about, say, a bowl of mocha chip.

9 Go to a masquerade ball (traditionally scheduled around Halloween, Mardi Gras, and the Carnivale seasons). Dressing up isn't just for kids. There's nothing like slipping into a costume to try out a new persona. You may not be ready to actually act out your sexual fantasies, but you can at least access your inner dominatrix or princess while he can play at being your little devil.

10 One way to jolt a little of the unknown into your same-old, same-old dates is to take turns planning a hush-hush romantic "mystery night." One of you makes all the arrangements and just tells the other where and when you'll meet. (You'll be surprised yourself by how much fun it can be to be the one orchestrating the night.) You can make a midday call or leave a love note where you know your partner will find it (in a lunch bag or briefcase, scribbled on the kids' Magna Doodle, in the car on the driver's seat, or propped against the milk in the refrigerator). The destination can be anything from a dinner at a nice restaurant to a scavenger hunt with you as the prize. It's not the venue that makes the evening special but the anticipation of not knowing what to expect.

GETTING HIM MOTIVATED FOR ROMANCE

One of the differences between newlyweds and "oldly-weds" is that people who've been an item for a while usually stop surprising each other. It's not that you're no longer capable of being unpredictable; it's just that it takes time to amaze when you know each other so well.

But what if your guy isn't really the kind of guy to spring a surprise romantic night on you? Sure, he's bowled you over with flowers a few times, maybe the occasional unexpected chocolate (although it still had the Hershey's wrapper). But a full-out every-detail-meticulously-planned-to-make-you-go-*awww* evening out? Never!

This doesn't mean that you aren't adored. It may just be that his idea of what constitutes a romantic surprise is different from yours. Maybe he parks his car on the street so you can get out easily in the morning. Perhaps he always buys strawberry ice cream because he knows it's your favorite even though he really prefers cookie dough. In his mind, these sweet little touches are just as unexpected and significant as organizing all the nitty-gritties of a razzle-dazzle wingding date. When you get right down to it, planning a romantic surprise, however big or small, is just shorthand for saying "I love you. I think about you. I am paying attention to who you are."

Of course, this warm fuzzy feeling may not be enough to cut it when you want to find a love poem in your wallet, to be serenaded at dinner and the whole extravagant nine yards. So tell him what you find romantic. Just say it outright. Coyness and suggestiveness may not serve you well with a nonromantic. Make it clear what you like, and there will be no room for confusion. Some men don't do romantic things because they think their idea will fail or you won't like it. (And chances are, if his imagination does not run toward the romantic surprise, his idea of what might be a fun surprise may run toward what would tickle *him* pink—nipple tassles, anyone?—and not necessarily what will make *you* shout "Whoopee!") Let him know what you like, and he'll feel safe enough to do it. So there probably won't be a violinist standing by the next time he brings you tea in bed, but there may just be candlelight and flowers.

And be prepared to be kind. Just because he did go all out doesn't mean that everything will be perfect. Nor does it mean you still won't have a good time. "Recently, my husband surprised me with tickets to a symphonic concert for my birthday," says Frannie, 30. "Usually, I am not thrilled about going out when it means getting dressed a little better then going to the movies or a local diner. But I got dressed up and, I might add, I looked pretty good. And then we had a horrible time. The concert was awful. But it didn't really matter. The night was still great because we ended up laughing about how bad the players were and enjoying each other's company . . . and later on, enjoying each other!"

The funny—read "frustrating"—thing about the difference between the sexes is that men complain that they have to do all the dirty work when it comes to keeping the spark alive between the sheets and women moan that they have to make all the effort when it comes to keeping things fiery outside of the bedroom. So, as for surprising *him,* dropping the little bombshell that you want him here and now will probably astonish and delight him.

These unexpected love moments will also make his heart melt. Before you try these, make sure he doesn't first make alternate plans. Then lower his expectations by telling him that you've made a dreary-sounding appointment (your parents are in town) that he won't dare to miss. You've prepared him mentally for a dull, dutiful evening, then you spring your romantic surprise. He'll be so relieved he can't help but have a good time.

- Give him a fifties night. Make sure you are home before him so you can freshen up. Put on a daytime dress and makeup and finish the look with a strand of pearls or a simple locket. Greet him when he walks through the door with a martini and a smile and a peck. If you have kids, make sure they are banished from the premises. Have dinner waiting on the table and then after the meal, bring him the paper and the remote. Massage his feet while he channel-surfs to his heart's content. At around nine P.M., smile coyly and tell him you are just going to freshen up. Slip into some girly pink lingerie and coo to him to come and join you for a romp.

- Tell him he has to do everything you say for an entire day. Start by taking him window shopping in the electronics section of a store. Then hit his favorite sports bar for snacks and a beer before going to a movie you know he will love but you normally wouldn't choose. Finish with a sexual position he has hinted he'd like to try (you know, the one that sounds sort of interesting but there never seems to be enough time to make it happen).

- Dress up like a fairy godmother, complete with wings and wand and tell him that you will grant him three wishes. No reneging!

PICKUP DATES

No plan? No problem. Here are four last-minute dates, no forethought required.

1 Do whatever it is you usually do on a date and then make it different. For instance, go ahead and go to a movie, but make it an X-rated one. Or eat out, but choose a cuisine that you've never tried (and frankly, has always seemed a bit too strange for you to try). For Lisa, 40, the twist was going on her usual mountain-biking date with her husband, Scott, but ending it with a skinny dip in a nearby pond. "Now we make it a point to map out rides near water," she says.

2 Take a tour of garage/moving/tag sales in the ritziest neighborhoods. Allot yourselves $20 each to spend however you want (you can pool your resources or buy something for yourselves or a surprise gift for each other).

3 Crash a wedding. Seeing two people take vows can make you gooey with love. You can usually stroll right in if the ceremony is taking place at a place of worship (but dress appropriately and stay near the back).

4 Have a midafternoon cuddle date. There's a lot to be said for stopping in your busy tracks in the middle of the day and tuning into each other. Chances are, those in-sync feelings will carry you through the rest of the day and well into the night, making it much easier to slip into a romantic bedtime mood. So turn off the phone, draw the blinds, and snuggle in each other's arms for a few hours. (This works well if you have a child who still naps at home.)

REAL-STEAL DEALS

These thrills cost less than your daily double-espresso latte, but they have a longer-lasting jolt.

- Take a stroll through a house you'd (someday) love to own. Check out the real estate listings for weekend open houses so you don't have to deal with a hard sell from the agent.

- Go on a free tour of a local factory. Not only is it fun to watch other people at work, it also can be a kick to discover what goes into making your favorite candy or exactly how a motorcycle is put together (think of the dinner-party-conversation material you can gather). Check with your local chamber of commerce or to find a tour near you go to factorytoursusa.com.

- You think *your* life is crazy? Spend the day at one of these weird and wild festivals: mashed-potato wrestling, a chicken-plucking competition, a wife carrying match, a cardboard boat race, or a watermelon seed-spitting contest. Flip through the listings page in your local paper or, for an overview of bizarre goings-on nationwide, check out eccentricamerica.com (also available in book format).

- Check out your local performance-art scene. The shows are rarely sold out, and you never know what bizarre spectacle you might be treated to—or asked to take part in. "My husband and I went to this show where we were told to throw cream pies at the actors. It was hilarious and, somehow, art!" laughs Anne, 45.

• See if there is a Renaissance Faire in your area. Enjoy the jugglers, jousts, tankards of ale, and turkey legs the size of your thigh. Challenge each other to talk in fake British accents the whole day.

DATING DILEMMAS

It's one of Cupid's practical jokes that in marriage, where you should feel safest about taking a risk, you actually feel at your most vulnerable. Here's what can go awry (and probably will) and how to make it right without losing out on what these screwball dates are all about: intimacy, communication, knowledge, and a huge wallop of passion.

Dilemma #1 •:
The date is more weird experience than wild fun.

Sometimes, something that sounds like a great idea doesn't quite make it in reality. Don't let the miscalculation stop you from trying and trying again. Half of the fun of taking a risk and doing something different is finding yourselves in a situation you didn't expect. The other half is how you handle it. If you both agree that going luging in the nude or whatever it was that you planned wasn't quite the giggle-a-minute thrill you had envisioned, skip the blamefest (even if it was his idea, you did agree to it). So chalk it down to a *c'est la vie* moment and move on.

Dilemma #2:

One of you thinks that this date is the best thing you have done since your first kiss; the other thinks even going to the dentist would rank higher on the amusement scale.

Expect to have different ideas of fun. This has nothing to do with how healthy your marriage is. According to REDBOOK Love Network expert John Gottman, Ph.D., compatibility in a relationship isn't all it's chalked up to be. While a certain amount of mutual understanding certainly helps smooth the edges of your union, it's not nearly as important as respect, acceptance, emotional connection, and communication. So the conflict isn't over whether you see eye to eye on what adds spice to a date; it's how you communicate your differing opinions. You need to be able to put new ideas out there without worrying about being judged or criticized. Agree to adopt a try-anything-once attitude: As long as no one is going to get hurt, you'll both give the experience a whirl and then decide after whether you want a replay. Chances are, once you create a climate of acceptance, you'll see that you have a lot more common ground that you realize.

Then again, some things are just too weird to do. For example:

• Joining him and the guys or having him crash your gal pal night. A nice way to give each other insight into your respective genders? It's more likely to give you nightmares. (He doesn't want to know how much you and your friends discuss sex, and you don't want to know how little he and his friends discuss sex.)

- Going to an orgy or swing party. Obviously, there are exceptions to every rule, but unless you are both completely on board with this little tryst on the wild side, this date will end in tears.

- Having quickie sex in a conspicuous place. Warning: If you're caught in flagrante delicto, the best you can hope for is feeling embarrassed and being asked to stop what you're doing and move along. But your little indiscretion could lead to a fine or even an arrest, especially if you get cozy near where children play.

Dilemma #3:
He makes his own plans (and they don't include you).

You've spent the last month planning a surprise night out that includes dinner at a restaurant notorious for its exclusivity (and jammed reservation lines), expensive tickets at a sold-out show, and a room at a hotel with a noncancellation policy only to have lover boy come home and casually inform you that all of his buddies from work are dropping by to catch the game, and, oh yeah, they just ordered a pizza. Go ahead and scream—privately—and then let the cat out of the bag and tell him, in the kindest tone possible, what is on the evening's agenda and that it most certainly does not include his "buds." Don't blast him for being inconsiderate. After all, how was he to know you had planned the date of the year? Next time (if, hopefully, there is one), ask him to set aside an evening for a romantic surprise. Rather than take away from the moment, hinting at what is to come will actually heighten the excitement by creating anticipation with a dollop of mystery.

outdoor
dates

Outdoor dates don't need to be just a summer affair. There's nothing like the sensual stimulation you let yourself in for just by being open to the everyday thrills of the world around you, whatever the forecast says: the cool touch of a breeze blowing gently against your skin, the heady aroma of pine needles blanketing a forest floor, the stunning sight and scent of a meadow full of wildflowers, the salty taste of the air at the beach, the lyrical sound of birds calling to their mates in the early morning, the miracle of watching the sun perform its daily light show. It's no surprise that all it takes are some natural conditions to make a person giddy with desire.

Each season offers its own unique romantic pleasures,

from licking the snowflakes off each other's faces during a winter stroll or cuddling up during a fall bonfire to bike riding through a spring shower or lazing all day in the summer sun.

So put this book down and head outside. Fresh air has always been good for you, but it's about to get a whole lot better.

TEN MUST-DO OUTDOOR DATES THAT'LL WAKE UP YOUR ROMANCE

If your idea of getting back to nature is watching the weather channel, chill; you don't have to cling to a mountainside or white-knuckle your way downriver to get turned on naturally. A romantic stroll, in all its down-to-earth splendor, can be enough to jump-start things. However, since the neighborhood circuit can get a little old after a while, here's how to move your date action outdoors (no training required).

1 Pack up a picnic. Whether in the wilderness, a local park, or your own backyard, dining al fresco provides a fabulous backdrop to your romance year round. Try these twists on the usual fare.

- Don't let the cold weather put a chill on your outdoor plans. Throw on an extra layer of clothes and fire up your meal on a mini grill or have a little campfire and toast marshmallows. Skip the wine and bring a Thermos of adult hot chocolate (spiked with rum and a pinch of cinnamon). Stay out long enough to watch the winter moon rise.

• Spice It Up •

Get your blood flowing with a snowball fight.

- If the only thing holding you back from taking your meal outside is the thought of a creepy crawly on your leg, take to the sky. What could be more romantic than picnicking up, up, and away in a beautiful balloon? Click on PartyPop.com for nationwide listings of hot-air balloon companies.

- Throw together a fall brown bagger of hot soup and cider and go kite flying on a windy hilltop. (Make sure there are no trees or electric power lines to get tangled up in.) See who can loop-de-loop the highest.

- If you can't get away from the house or don't have the time to put together a picnic meal, bring the action to your backyard. Just pick up the phone and order a pizza, some Chinese appetizers, or whatever kind of food that is available in your hamlet. Ask the person to bring your food straight around the house into your yard. Make the setting more romantic with Christmas lights, small candles, and the boom box softly playing your favorite tunes.

- Most mornings, you don't have time to stop and smell the roses. So this Sunday, set your alarm for an early wake-up call and then head out to a spot where you can have a picnic breakfast while watching the sun come up. The night before, pack chocolate croissants (buy a can of refrigerated crescent roll dough and press some chocolate chips into the center before baking), berries, yogurt packs, and a Thermos each of hot coffee and mimosas (Champagne mixed with freshly squeezed OJ). Enjoy your day.

2 Find a dark spot away from the lights and go stargazing. Pick up a book on astronomy and see how many constellations and planets you can identify. *A Child's Introduction to the Night Sky: The Story of the Stars, Planets, and Constellations—and How You Can Find Them in the Sky* by Michael Driscoll (Black Dog & Leventhal Publishers, 2004) and *Spotters Guide to the Night Sky* by Nigel Henbest and Stuart Atkins (Usborne Books, 2000) were both written for children, but that just means that the language is easy to understand and more fun to read than a serious scientific tome.

• S p i c e   I t   U p •

You don't have to shell out fifty bucks for the pleasure of having your own private star. Just pick a point of light in the sky and name it. Mark its location (where it lives among the constellations) and make a monthly date to see if you can find it again (download a sky map of your location at fourmilab.ch/yoursky).

3 Cure your cabin fever and spend the entire day outside. Having a full day to play in the great outdoors is a luxury in this busy world, where weekends are usually taken up by laundry, grocery shopping, chauffeuring, and other humdrum household chores. And an active adventure in nature can lead to bigger, grander conversations than the usual how-your-week-was recitals. Here's how to blow some fresh air into your lives:

- Lay new tracks on some just fallen snow.
- Inflate a float and drift and dream the day away in a pool or small pond.
- Dig a flower garden.
- Find a patch of grass where you can cuddle up together and exchange sweet nothings.
- Go for an all-day hike (check out trails.com for a listing of nearby treks).
- Rent a bicycle built for two (you'll be surprised how much teamwork it requires to get anywhere).
- Go for an off-season meander along the beach (don't forget to build a sand castle).
- Instead of a leaf-drive, try a leaf-bike, -foot or -horse ride.

4 Check out your local nature show. No matter where you live, Mama Nature has something special up her sleeve, from live volcanoes to glowing jellyfish. Your state's Audubon Society (Main Office: National Audubon Society, 700 Broadway, New York, NY 10003, Phone: (212) 979-3000, Web site: audubon.org) will have the skinny on natural phenomena in your area, but there are some seasonal shows that are not so site specific. Check out who or what may be touring in your area soon (log on to learner.org for details on animal migration paths).

- **BIRD WATCHING:** Lovebirds can grab a pair of binoculars and a field guide any time of the year and spend an afternoon finding out who is on your current flight path.

- **BUTTERFLIES:** Summer is the best time to spy most of these winged insects, but watch out for the majestic annual southern trek of the Monarch butterfly in the fall.

- **BABY ANIMALS:** Visit the zoo in the spring to see the results of how the mama and papa beasts of the wild spent their winter vacation.

- **WHALE WATCHING:** Talk about being picky about your nooky environment. Whales must migrate every year from cool feeding locations to warmer climates in order to breed. December and January are the best months for West Coast sightings while East Coasters will have better luck in the spring.

- **SEAL WATCHING:** If you live near the northern coast, you may be able to check out a family of these marine mammals taking in the afternoon sun on an outcrop of rocks.

- **FISH RUN:** If you think your sex life has problems, pity the poor fish who must battle against currents between mid-spring to mid-summer to spawn. Look for herrings on the East Coast, salmon on the West Coast and striped bass throughout the United States.

• S p i c e I t U p •

Take a leisurely trip to the nearest field, spread a blanket, and count how many lightning bugs appear. Mimic their mating dance by kissing every time you spot one.

5 Get rocking. Go on a gem-hunting hike. It doesn't matter if that pebble you find really is quartz (one of the most popular minerals) instead of a diamond. It's special to you because it will always remind you of this day. If you live near a beach, look for a beautiful shell or piece of sea glass.

• S p i c e I t U p •

Take your special find and have it fitted for a necklace or ring. (Who needs precious gems?)

6 Spend an evening on the water. Rent a rowboat for a DIY sunset cruise and dinner. (Tip: You can keep your drinks cold by tying a rope around the bottle neck or using a net to carry them and trailing the whole kit and caboodle behind you in the water as you head for the middle of the lake). Pack a blanket and sit back and watch for the stars to appear. Don't forget to make a wish.

• S p i c e I t U p •

Bring along a couple of fishing poles and see if you can catch dinner.

7 Camping is a great way to smoke some fire into a relationship. Nothing is boring because everything is different. Even the most common and everyday tasks, such as cooking, sleeping, or going to the bathroom, become adventuresome. There's no TV to interrupt your conversation, and the nights are long, so you can retire early to your sleeping bags (zipped together, of course).

However, the very thing that makes camping such a bonding affair—the need to learn how to survive as a couple—can also make it a tense, tight-lipped experience if you can't deal when the going gets tough, and it will; stones have an unexpected way of popping up on smooth ground just as you are trying to go to sleep, fires go out before dinner is cooked, bears may make unexpected house calls because, *ahem,* one of you forgot to put away the trash . . . Here are a few tips to keep your relationship from roughing it:

- Never make a hammock chair do more than what it was born to do.
- You always get the warmer jacket, even if it's his.
- Instant sterilizing hand lotion is not a luxury.
- When you're carrying gear, don't try to evenly distribute the weight. Men carry the heavier pack. It's been that way for thousands of years; don't fight the system.
- Pick a bundle of wildflowers and stick them in a cup: instant bouquet.
- If the fire keeps on going out, give up and make your own.
- Pledge to take a hot bath together when you get home.

While the great outdoors supplies plenty of natural romantic atmosphere (stars, moonlight, wooded copses, possibly a nearby waterfall or sandy nook, a campfire), you can still work the mood. Here's how to gear up for a romantic stint in the boonies. (The following equipment is available from most outfitters: Try REI at 1-800-426-4840 or rei.com, L.L. Bean at 1-800-441-5713 or llbean.com, and Summit Hut at summithut.com or 800-499-8696.)

- **A CANDLE LANTERN.** Better than the real thing because it doesn't blow out and unexpectedly leave you in the dark. The Uco Candlelier (around $35) is lightweight, while the more high-tech GSI Shaker Lantern (around $64), which has a dimmer switch, will add a dash of romantic ambience to your campsite.

- **AN IPOD:** Of course, you can just listen to the night sounds, but if you want to amplify your love tunes (and tune out the sound of lions and tigers and bears— oh my!—creeping around the underbrush), an iPod is easier to carry than a portable CD and holds enough tunes for you to put on your own private concert.

- **CAMOUFLAGE LINGERIE:** Wear these outdoor undies (found at hunting-supply stores), and you'll blend right in with your surroundings. Perfect for playing hanky-panky hide-'n'-seek.

- **TENT:** Get a big one. You want to be sure of plenty of room for any, *ahem,* twisting and turning. A few tents in the plus-size range: The Big Agnes Parkview 2 Tent ($300), Mountain Hardwear Light Wedge 2

Tent ($200), and Marmot Mercury Tent ($300) are all lightweight, three-season, and boast lots of square footage to romp in.

- **SLEEPING BAGS:** Since sleeping separately defeats the purpose and trying to squeeze together in a single sleeping bag will defeat sexual logistics, spring for a sleeping system that accommodates doubling up. Mountain Hardwear Duet Coupler (around $65), The North Face Cat's Meow bags (around $170 each), and Marmot Wasatch bags (around $200 each) all have features that make it easy to snuggle up.

Perhaps the thought of sleeping on the ground makes your heart palpitate more from the fear of being so close to nature than from the excitement of getting down and dirty with your partner. You don't have to go far. Just pitching a tent in your backyard will take you away from it all.

• S p i c e   I t   U p •

Take along a few hair-raising stories to read together while snuggling under the covers. *Casting the Runes and Other Ghost Stories* (Oxford World's Classics, 2002) edited by M. R. James and Michael Cox (Oxford University Press, 1999), *The Best Ghost Stories Ever* edited by Christopher Krovatin (Scholastic Paperbacks, 2004), and any selection from the *Scary Stories* series edited by Alvin Schwartz (HarperCollins) will all have you shaking in your boots (and grasping for each other in the dark).

8 Get drunk on love. Have a grape escape and pedal though a vineyard, sampling the local vintages (biking means you avoid the need for a designated driver). Pack some cheese and crackers and find a winery near you. Not sure where to find one? Go to chiff.com/wine/n-america/USA.htm. If you prefer to raise a stein, look in your local paper around October for beer festivals or click on allaboutbeer.com or beersweetbeer.com to find a draft-brewing in your area.

9 Make hay during harvest time with these days out in the country:

- Put on your overalls and head over to a country fair. There is something down-home romantic about spending the day sharing candy apples, and corn dogs, checking out the prizewinning cows and pigs; winning an ugly troll at a ringtoss; doing a round of do-si-do at a square dance; and ending the evening on a high note with a kiss on top of the Ferris wheel. Find a fair near you at honeymoons.about.com/cs/activeadventures/a/statefair_2.htm or check with your local co-operative extension office or 4-H Club.

- Call out a great big *yee haw* and hightail it over to a rodeo show. What could be more fun than watching cowboys in (tight) Wranglers and cowhide chaps wrestling 600-pound steers, and anxious gals, resplendent in sequined gowns, hoping they're the one crowned queen? Check out prorodeo.com or rodeo.about.com for a bucking-bronco show near you.

- The average tomato travels around 1,500 miles to land in your salad. Join a Community Supported Agriculture (CSA), where you'll be able to pick up (and sometimes pick) farm fresh, locally grown, often organic produce, fruits, flowers, eggs, milk, meats, and sometimes even coffee on a weekly or monthly basis during the growing season. Make it a regular date and after, you can head home and cook up a romantic meal together. To find a CSA farm near you, log on to local harvest.org/csa.

- Go for a hayride at twilight. Climb into the back of a covered wagon or old truck, and don't restrain yourself from cuddling up and bouncing on his lap.

- Spend the day nibbling each other's fruits. Depending on where you live, you can pick your own apples, peaches, berries, melons, pumpkins, citrus, and flowers; press apple cider; or tap your own maple syrup. (The co-operative extension office in your community will be able to tell you which farms and orchards let you play Farmer Brown for the day.)

• Spice It Up •

If you've been cavorting in a pumpkin patch, don't throw away the seeds after carving up your gourd. Instead, turn them into a snack: Rinse in cold water, pat dry, sprinkle with salt, drizzle with olive oil, and bake them at 350°F on a baking sheet for thirty minutes. The pumpkin-y scent will arouse more than his tastebuds, so don't be surprised if he wants to skip the snack and head straight to the sack.

10 Warm each other up with a faux sauna. Roll around naked in the snow and then head (read "rush") inside for a warm bath *à deux.* Or challenge each other to a Polar Bear Plunge taking place near you. Many states hold this event on the chilliest days of winter (usually as a charity fund-raiser). Don't stay in longer than fifteen minutes, or hypothermia may set in. There may be heated tents on hand or head straight home to have your own personal thaw-out.

PICKUP DATES

No plan? No problem. Here are four last-minute dates, no forethought required.

1 The first day of summer (usually around June 21) boasts the most hours of sunlight in a day. Midsummer, as the day is called, is thought to hold a special magic for lovers (Shakespeare's play *A Midsummer Night's Dream* is based on this concept). Celebrate with an all-day date. Wake early to watch the sunrise together. If possible, spend the day outdoors and together. Regardless, though, make sure you meet up to watch the sunset arm in arm.

2 On a crispy fall day, go grave rubbing. Start at an art supply store and pick up some construction paper, masking tape, charcoal crayons, and metallic gold and silver crayons. Find the oldest cemetery in your area (they have the most romantic inscriptions and the most ornate decorations). When you find a stone you like, tape the paper over the inscription and rub the broad side of the crayon over the inscription. Instant art! You can frame your masterpiece and hang it when you get home.

• Spice It Up •

Pack up a sleeping bag, a flashlight, and a Thermos of hot cider and stay at the cemetery past dark. Spook yourselves silly telling ghost stories.

3 Warm up on a winter day ice skating at an outdoor rink. Few things are more romantic than gliding along holding hands on the frozen ice and helping each other up with a feel-better kiss after the inevitable fall. Finish with a massage to soothe your tired muscles.

4 Sex in the rain can be erotic and sensual, as long as it's a warm shower (cold water causes his delicates to shrink). Inhale the earthy sweetness of the storm and let the water cascade over your bodies as you embrace and connect not only with each other but with nature as well. After, chase rainbows.

REAL-STEAL DEALS

These dates are free all year long.

- Train together to compete in a race. A little friendly rivalry can be good for your relationship. You stimulate, energize, and spur each other on to do more and be more while working toward a common goal (to ensure that harmony reigns, always go at the slower person's pace). How you work out together can also be a clue to how you are together as a couple because you need listen to, compromise with, and anticipate each other's needs and abilities—and to stop without recrimination if one of you is driven to tears. The sweet payoff (besides getting fit): Getting sweaty with your partner gives you both a better understanding of each other's bodies, not a bad thing for after-workout workouts in the bedroom.

- Go on a bird-feeding expedition at a park with a lake. Take along stale bread or crackers for the ducks and a Thermos of homemade lemonade or iced tea (spiked) for the two of you. See if you can spot the pairs.

- Grab a basketball and hit the free courts at the park for a game of one-on-one (make the penalties X rated!).

- Laugh like a five-year-old and play at the playground. See who can swing the highest.

- Create a work of art together. Pick up a paint-by-numbers kit and do it like the impressionists by working on your masterpiece outside.

DATING DILEMMAS

Mother Nature can be treacherous and unpredictable. Here's how to deal when she throws a temper tantrum.

Dilemma #1
It's too hot/cold/buggy/wet/foggy/smoggy/snowy/ fill-in-the- blank to go outside.

Don't let unexpected weather conditions put a damper on your date.

Four Hot Things You Can Do in the Snow

1. Have a snowball fight. The "loser" makes a romantic dinner.

2. Forget about building a snowman. Instead, create your own private art show by carving different shapes out of the snow (heart, cat, castle).

3. With a Thermos filled with hot cocoa and a sled built for two, head for the steepest hill you can find and go sledding (remember to kiss all "I-fell-off-and-bonked-my-head" boo-boos).

4. Practice Eskimo kisses.

Four Wet-and-Wild Things You Can Do in the Rain

1. Take a squishy barefoot walk around the block (leave the umbrella at home).

2. Play touch football with as little clothing as possible.

3. Drive to your local inspiration point and steam up the windows.

4. Head outside and slow-dance to the pitter-patter of the raindrops.

Four Cool Things to Do When It's Too Darned Hot

1. Run through the sprinklers (bonus: wet T-shirt contest!).

2. Have a naked day.

3. Melt down with an ice-cube all-over rub.

4. Cover each other in ice cream and lick it off.

Three Weather-Proof Things You Can Do Whenever

1. Have a picnic on your porch, in your car, under a lean-to, or (build-your-own) snow fort.

2. Drive to the next town and see what the weather is like there.

3. Bask in the heat of a bonfire. You don't have to be a wilderness grizzly to master building a fire in bad weather. All you need are waterproof matches and these quick steps:

- Crumple some newspaper or make a small pile of pine needles or bark to use as your fire starter.

- Use small twigs to build a tepee over your fire starter.

- Carefully lay larger branches on top of your twig tepee.

- Light the fire starter.

- As the fire starts to burn, add more twigs and branches, keeping to the tepee shape.

- Make sure you douse all embers with sand, dirt, or water when you are finished, even if it's pouring rain. All it takes is one small runaway spark to make a fire go out of control.

Check out the weather in advance. At weather. com, you can get the forecast, UV index, daylight hours remaining, a mosquito-activity forecast and a Picnic and Grilling Index that rates the appropriateness of the days' weather for outdoor plans.

Dilemma #2

Your raunchy romp outside was a little too close to nature for your liking.

Here's how to avoid the pitfalls of al fresco sex next time (assuming there is one!):

- Mosquitoes love moist, dark places; you get the picture *(ouch!)*. Spray yourselves with repellent before heading out. When camping, bring bug-repelling citronella candles. A blanket or sleeping bag will also serve as a barrier between you and any creepy crawlies.

- Poison ivy, oak, and sumac can be found on the ground, twining up a tree, even at the beach. These plants also look different, depending on the season (a scroll through poisonivy.aesir.com will give you a year-round picture

I.D.). If you do encounter one, wash the sap off your body and clothes immediately. While most dermatologists agree that scratching by itself won't spread the rash, the superpotent sap will. Take an antihistamine and, on nongenital areas, apply calamine lotion to dry out the rash. If you do have a reaction in your vaginal area, call a doctor right away—you may need a cortisone pill or shot—and, in the meantime, apply 1 percent hydrocortisone cream (available over the counter) to relieve the discomfort.

- Water seems like a wet place for sex, but it can actually wash away your own natural lubrication and dry out your lovemaking. Water can also get forced into your vagina and lead to infection. While the H_2O seems crystal clear to the eye, it may be teeming with microbes that can cause an infection. Even chlorinated water can disrupt your body's healthy bacteria and change the natural pH (acidity) in the vagina, leading to a yeast infection. So be safe and keep your underwater adventures above the waist. Also be on the watch for stinging jellyfish and avoid playing where there is snorkeling action.

- Your genitals are basically virgin skin because they are rarely exposed to outdoor light, so take care not to give them too much fun in the sun. (Warning: The oils in sunscreens can eat holes in latex contraception like diaphragms and condoms.)

- Sand can get into the creases and folds of the vagina, causing abrasions. If you get a sand burn, clean the area with cold water and don't have sex again until you're completely healed (a few days to a week). Next time, use a blanket.

- The outdoor motto is leave nothing but footprints or, in this case, body prints. Smooth down dirt or sand mounds, rearrange flora, and try to make the area look like it did before you came. Also remember to collect all of your debris before leaving your sex nook.

Dilemma #3

You couldn't find a comfortable position to cavort in outside.

Memorize this all-purpose position for every environment: Stand facing each other. Lift your leg and move it slightly to the side so he can penetrate you. Once he's inside of you, he can lift you by placing his hands under your thighs while you wrap your arms around his neck to keep your balance.

Chapter 9

ILLUMINATING
DATES

Ask yourself this: When was the last time you learned
something new together? Not because you *had* to
(like how to read your health-care benefits or the
breathing sequence of Lamaze) but because you really,
really wanted to?

Chances are, it was back in the day when you were
still a wet-behind-the-ears couple. It's not that you
don't want to get out there and challenge yourselves; it's
just that the everyday details of life have this annoying
tendency to get in the way of more interesting and lofty
pursuits. But mental stimluation is not something that
should get shoved to the bottom of your list. Partially
because *learning* together gets you *doing* together, no
small feat in the busy whirl of life. Forging this sort of

connection also stops your relationship from operating on autopilot. You stay on your toes and remain open to new ideas and ways of doing things (which, in turn, ensures that you have something to talk about on your dates for the next fifty years or so!).

Just one thing: Be daring! You don't have to resort to skydiving or bungee jumping. But instead of automatically nixing the stuff that doesn't appeal, make a deal to try everything the other person wants to do at least once. You might just surprise yourself and develop some new interests. "The idea of me ballroom dancing made me shudder," says Terry, 32, who claims to not having danced in public since he was in a kindergarten production of "The Flight of the Bumble Bee." "But my wife got a coupon for a free class and begged me to go, saying it could be her Valentine's, birthday, and anniversary present that year. It turned out that the class was mostly beginners, which helped. I ended up really getting into the music and not tripping once. And when we got home, we were both eager to continue the date in bed! While we haven't returned to that class, I have tried other dance classes with her and found I really love to salsa. And I still got her presents on the special dates."

Here are some hot new pursuits guaranteed to breathe fresh air into your relationship.

TEN MUST-DO DATES
TO KEEP YOU OPEN-MINDED

You don't have to pick each other's brains for nights out that will teach you something new. Best yet, many of these dates are inexpensive, time flexible, and don't require hours of intensive commitment. Translation: They can easily be worked into even the most cramped schedule or combined with a multitude of follow-up activities, such as grabbing a bite to eat or—now that you're all fired up—some love lessons with your honey.

1 Art is a hot topic. The reason artists create in the first place is to get viewers thinking about what they are seeing. You may not like it or even think you don't understand it, but that just makes for a better conversation. And art exhibits are everywhere, so it's easy to organize a date around one. Almost every metropolitan area, regardless of size or geography, has an art museum or a collection on view in a public space. Larger cities often have several that specialize in the art of different eras or regions. Colleges and universities usually have art available as well, sometimes in their administrative and classroom buildings. Banks, libraries, even public schools are often hosting some sort of exhibit. If you're not sure where to find the paintings, sculptures, or photographs near you, look in the newspaper or in a community guide or do an online search (museumstuff.com has links to thousands of art institutions in America and abroad; the Art Museum Network at amn.org lists an exhibition calendar of the world's leading art museums; and galleryguide.org will help you easily locate an art venue near you).

Know that there is no wrong and right when it comes to what you like about a piece of work. But askart.com will give you the basics on art terms, artists, and art movements to help get you in the scene for some postviewing discussion over a glass of wine.

2 If art really isn't your thing, a museum in your area may be offering an exhibit on the history of hockey, fashion design through the ages, or strange surgical equipment. Or there may be a specialty museum in your area that focuses on a specific passion like trains, food, or sex (look in your local Yellow Pages under "Museums" to see what's in your neighborhood).

• Spice It Up •

If the above aren't enough of a conversation starter, then how about a vibrator chair? Or fantasy coffins? There are weird and wacky museums offering exhibits on everything from human body parts to funeral history to everything you never knew you needed to know about mustard. One good source for the weird and wacky is museumspot.com. Or look in your local newspaper under gallery listings.

3 Work up a sweat together with your clothes on, but skip the jogging and aerobics and try an activity that doesn't rely on brawn to succeed, such as fencing, orienteering, rock climbing, and adventure racing. This way, you'll start out on a level playing field.

• S p i c e   I t   U p •

You can massage each other's sore muscles later that night.

4 Nurture your inner artist. Go to a create-your-own ceramics store and paint each other's image or favorite thing on his-'n'-her mugs (just make sure there are no birthday parties planned for that day). Once your artwork is ready, wrap them up as morning-after gifts. You'll be reminded of your romance every time you drink your morning brew.

• S p i c e   I t   U p •

Take a hint from Demi and Patrick in the film *Ghost* and get all hot and bothered while throwing your own pottery. Clay has a really sexy texture that gets you feeling all fired up.

5 Teach each other something. Remember, when you first combusted as a couple, how he melted when you taught him how to change a tire or how you couldn't stop gushing when he showed you a killer opening chess move? There's nothing like being appreciated for some specific smarts to make a person feel like hot stuff. Everyone has his or her own special talent, be it knowing how to order wine, read a map, identify the bug lurking in the bathroom, play the stock market, knit a hat; take turns making teaching dates to share your specific knowledge with each other. It doesn't really matter if you are a star pupil. This is more about appreciating what makes you different than mastering a new skill.

• S p i c e   I t   U p •

Instead of gold stars, hand out kisses.

6 Sign up to take a music lesson together. It doesn't matter if your instrument of choice is the harmonica or the accordion. You may not end up playing symphonies, but you will probably be able to still make beautiful music together. According to research by psychologist Raymond Macdonald of the British Society of Music Therapy, making music can actually improve your conversation skills because it gets you talking in a new way. To find a teacher look on the notice board at your local music store or ask the teacher at your local high school for recommendations.

• S p i c e   I t   U p •

Get all dolled up and catch an orchestra or opera performance.

7 Revisit what you think you already know. Spend an afternoon test-driving cars, viewing model homes, or window-shopping. Even if you have no interest in making a purchase now, these activities can kick-start discussions about your goals. New lovers are always dreaming together about the things they want to achieve as a couple: exotic trips, houses, cars, children. As love matures, you become much more focused on the here and now—attending school meetings, making lunch, folding socks—and forget to write the next chapter of your love story or think you don't have to because you already discussed all this a few years ago. But continually setting goals together gives love something to reach for, work toward, shape itself around.

8 Do unto others. The term *charity date* may sound like something from your single days, but dedicating time at a soup kitchen, an animal shelter or a neighborhood garden can teach you about how you work as a team outside of your usual comfort zone. Plus the good feelings that come from working toward a common goal through a charity or a cause helps to strengthen your intimate bond.

Volunteering is also likely to make you feel good. According to one survey, almost half of the respondents said volunteering had helped their health and fitness, and a quarter of those who gave up their time at least five times a year also reported weight loss—not a bad benefit of giving back. To choose a good match, log on to volunteermatch.org or check your religious center for volunteer opportunities in your area.

9 Make a reservation at an organized coffee night, high tea, or, if offered in your area, a Japanese tea ceremony, where you sit and chat with other people while sampling different refreshments. These events usually include a host who guides the conversation, which spans everything from art and current events to travel and the Zen of rituals.

10 Go back to school. Discovering something new together propels you out of your comfort zone and adds a layer of emotional connection to your relationship that will last long after the class has ended. Here are a few possible out-of-the-ordinary passions to help keep you tight over time:

- Tantric Sex Workshop: These courses teach you "conscious" lovemaking, which helps you to become more aware of each other and to learn to revere each other in and out of bed.

- Couples Yoga: Twisting your body into pretzel poses will bring you closer together physically (besides, it's damned sexy); and the teamwork it requires will also reveal the dynamics of your relationship. (Leave time for a postclass discussion over a pot of green tea.)

- Dance Class: Even more important than mastering the tango and the waltz, you will learn how to work your bodies in sync as well as how to work together in your relationship. When you dance, one of you takes a step forward, and the other responds by taking a step back. When you lose your footing, you recover and dance on. When he spins you out, you know that you'll always come back together again. Bonus: You'll be one of those shameless couples at other people's weddings, out on the dance floor for every number. To spice it up, spend the evening dancing to your favorite tunes.

- Take a life-drawing class and then go home and sketch each other (in the nude).

- Try scuba lessons together. They may get you dreaming about running off for a mini getaway at a remote tropical island.

- Master American Sign Language. At the very least, you now have a silent way of exchanging secret messages of love.

- Learn a new foreign language and, if possible, start planning a romantic vacation to the country where the language is spoken.

Not sure where to find a class that will interest you? Try these locations:

- Community colleges, community centers like the Y, and the public library are great resources for continuing your education.
- Local public school systems often offer adult ed. classes (call the school board).
- Local shops may have class information (for instance, a health-food store might be able to tell you about Tantric classes).
- Three's a lot more going on at the gym besides aerobics; many offer a variety of dance and yoga classes.
- Rifle through your local newspaper for related club and group activities.

When all else fails:

- Score a video on the subject.
- Check out correspondence schools.
- Look for classes online.
- Check with affiliated groups to see if there are teaching videos on the subject.

PICKUP DATES

No plan? No problem. Here are four last-minute dates, no forethought required.

1 Become biologists-in-training. Pick an animal species or a theme and then head over to the zoo and find out as much as you can about your subject. (For instance, see how many animals fall under the listing "endangered species.") Then head over to the monkey cage and see if you can get them to make faces at you.

2 Skip the museum tour. Instead, pack a picnic and sketch pad and head to a scenic bluff to draw your own version of the vista.

3 For an atmosphere that's quiet and intimate (and company that's divine), go to a bookstore that has a café attached. Browse separately, picking up a stack of books to bring back to the coffee area (or a prearranged meeting point in the store). Try to keep the subjects browser friendly such as home improvements/decorating, inspirational, travel, art. Sit together and share your finds, taking turns reading paragraphs here and there, checking out the pictures, and discussing what you are looking at.

• Spice It Up •

Limit your choices to romantic poetry.

4 Pick up a challenging jigsaw puzzle at the toy store. You'll need to reason, deduce, analyze, and problem solve together. Or create your own love puzzle: At piczzle.com, you can turn your favorite digital photo into a wood or cardboard 1,800-piece puzzle; or go to amoredpenguin.com to customize your own word puzzle or jumble, using nicknames, locations that have a special memory, or whatever else springs to mind.

• Spice It Up •

When you finish an extra-difficult puzzle, glue it together and hang it to remind yourselves of what you have accomplished together.

REAL-STEAL DEALS

You don't have to set up a special savings fund for your relationship education. Here are frugal ways you can learn together.

- Check to see if there are any free music festivals going on in your neck of the woods. They often include a lecture or two by an educator in the field.

- If it takes a little black dress (and a little red wine) to put you in the mood, get yourself on the invitation lists of local art galleries. They usually serve complementary wine and hors d'oeuvres.

- Museums usually have one free night a week. (Many also have a suggested entrance fee; read the fine print.)

- Many of the bigger museums hold free socials on weekend nights. The live music, lite bites on offer, and wine bar create an elegant, loungelike atmosphere. You may have to pay extra to check out the exhibition (in case you really are there for the art!).

- For some of the highest-quality education you can get for free, search out a lecture series on a topic you're both interested in at universities and community colleges in the surrounding area.

- The Association of Alternative Weeklies (aan.org) has a database of city magazines with event listings for everything you might never have even known you wanted to do.

- Form your own private book club for two. Read the same books and spend the night at a local coffee shop discussing your thoughts.

- You don't have to be highbrow about your culture. Amateur theater is fun to see (and, if you have the time, even more fun to try out for). Colleges, towns, even local religious institutions have theater troupes.

- See if your liquor store hosts wine-tasting nights (it's only expensive if you buy). Cheers to you if you pull off vino vocab like "full-bodied" or "supple" with a straight face.

• S p i c e   I t   U p •

Many specialty stores hold tasting parties. Check out chocolate stores, cheese shops, ethnic food markets, or even health-food stores.

- Look around for bookstores, libraries, and societies that are having guest speakers for free. You never know what you'll learn.

- Master the constellations and never get lost at night again (seamen used to use the stars to guide them). If you have a planetarium nearby, do some stargazing at the evening show. Many amp up the glitz factor with laser shows set to rock tunes.

• Spice It Up •

See the real thing. There is nothing like watching a meteor shower together to make you get starry eyed about each other. Since these often take place very early in the morning (comets.amsmeteors.org has a calendar of astronomical events in your area), set your alarm, pack a Thermos of hot chocolate, and head to the nearest wide-open space. Hold hands while you watch the heavens light up. Or, if waking with the birds is not your idea of romance, take a backyard stroll under the next full moon.

DATING DILEMMAS

Sharing your passions can make you feel vulnerable. Yes, you know each freckle on his body and can predict what he is going to say before he even thinks it, but it is exactly this intimacy that makes it feel like such a risk to open up about the things that deeply move you. If it doesn't work out, it can feel like the ultimate rejection (think how you felt when your first boyfriend broke up with you because you were "too different" but only a thousand times worse, because this isn't some pimple-faced boy;

it's your one and only spouse). Here's how to stay open-minded whatever happens.

Dilemma #1
You tried it; you didn't like it.

Fine. If you don't have a compelling desire to share your partner's interest, you should still respect and honor the fact that this is something he values. Rather than just rejecting him outright, let him know that while gangsta rap may not be your musical cup of tea, you value his interest in it perhaps by picking up a new rap CD that you can listen to together in the car while off to dally in more mutually satisfying pursuits. You may even find that your initial negative reaction was really that resistance every busy person experiences when trying to squeeze something new into his or her life. Once the activity becomes part of your regular routine, you may even discover that you are—surprise, surprise—enjoying yourself.

Dilemma #2
You tried it, and you really, really hated it.

Do not, repeat *do not,* insist that your partner give up an activity because you dislike it, and don't give up something you love for him. While it's good to share interests (and you shouldn't stop trying to find something that makes both of your brains hum), you don't have to do everything together. If it turns out that he would sooner give up his monthly poker game with his buddies than learn French with you, so be it. Maybe he would be more open to going to a French brasserie with you and letting you do all the ordering. And you may just discover that you share a passion for learning how to cook the croque monsieur, escargots, or whatever fare you are eating. In successful relationships, couples accept that some differences are an inevitable part of life and figure out how to make them work. The thing is, sometimes we forget that simply spending time together doing those things your partner enjoys most is enough to make his day. Even if you know little about his interest, the fact that you choose to spend time with him doing his favorite thing can make him feel like you really are the most wonderful person in the world (in real terms, the equivalent of about two hundred no-time-limit back rubs).

Dilemma #3
One of you is better at it than the other.

Oh, get over it. So you kicked his kingly butt at chess. Or he remembers each artist's entire bio. You may not buy the experts' party line about taking pleasure in each other's accomplishments and empathizing over each other's losses, so try this on for size: A little light competition is generally healthy and can spur you on. To make sure that friendly competition doesn't turn vicious, agree to keep out any trash talk.

Dilemma #4
You don't get it.

Just because you don't understand what it is that is grabbing his interest doesn't mean you don't get him and vice versa. It just means you both have undiscovered depths. Sometimes, it helps to adjust your assumption about what it is that is turning your partner on. For instance, Lydia, 40, eye-rolled over her husband, Frank's, passion for soccer while he thought her love of theater was boring. But after a few thousand hours' worth of discussion on the subject, they finally figured out that the two activities were more similar than they realized: Both involved drama and an interaction of players that could affect the action. "He doesn't go to every play with me and I don't attend all the matches, but it's a lot more fun now that we understand what the other person is getting out of it," she says.

Chapter 10

MINI GETAWAYS

S ometimes you don't need to just get out of the house; you need to get out of your life and away from unloading the dishwasher, driving the kids to the dentist, taking care of work business, mowing the grass, feeding the cat, dog, and guinea pig, saying hello to neighbors, cooking dinner, talking to your mom on the phone, and the 1,001 other everyday pressures and distractions that make up your day. When you're overtired, overworked, or under stress, you just don't have the desire or the energy to focus on each other.

A romantic retreat isn't just a change of scenery; it's a change of mind. Getting away from it all helps get you back to that place you were when you first got together and it was just the two of you on your own little island of love and desire. When your usual daily routine is not part of the itinerary, you'll find time for things you once enjoyed but abandoned to make way for more pressing endeavors. High on this list is sex. Sex out of the bedroom. Sex at any hour and duration. And sex at yes, yes, yes, any volume. But also for less carnal diversions like spending the day at a museum or sleeping until noon or having ice cream for dinner because that's what you both feel like doing.

Maybe you don't have the time, money, or ability to run away together for a couple of days. No excuses. Become a day-tripper instead. Grab your love and head for the hills or the next town over or even the hotel down the block. Where or how long you go isn't as important as departing from your daily routine so that you can spend time together truly connecting.

Best of all, the sizzle needn't fizzle once you get back home. Taking time off together reminds you of what your relationship is missing: quality bonding time, the kind that keeps you feeling weak-at-the-knees giddy about each other. Yes, it's hard to make the effort to cut yourself off from outside pressures at certain times in the evening or on the weekends, but think of it as taking a trip while staying at home. After nine P.M., for example, take the phone off the hook and turn off the computer. You don't have to instantly jump into bed. But when you have a chance to be alone together with no distractions, that's where you'll probably want to be.

Read on for your road map to blissful breaks that you can easily pack into your travel plans.

TEN MUST-DO
GREAT ESCAPE DATES

Give in to your romantic wanderlust for a few hours or even a few days with these quick getaways.

1 Take him to the town where you grew up and take a stroll around your old haunts, sharing memories. If possible, include a visit to your old after-school hangout and make out like crazy-in-lust teenagers.

2 Go on a road trip to a nearby town where no one knows you. Make the most of your anonymity by ditching your usual couple character. You can make believe that you're from another country and don't speak English and try to chat with the locals. Or pretend that you're lovers on an illicit tryst and act just-this-side-of-the-law indecently (sit on his lap while eating lunch, kiss outrageously on street corners, walk arm in arm no matter how crowded the street). Access your inner stylist and dress up in a way that you never would in your own neighborhood. Or try the hair color you always wanted with a wig or wash-in/wash-out shampoo. Get childish at the playground on the swings and slides. Taking a risk together, even a silly one, adds a new dynamic to your relationship that lasts long after your hair returns to its usual shade.

3 Visit a country where neither of you speaks the language. There is nothing like being in a place where you can't even say good morning in the local lingo to instantly redefine your shared identity as a couple and make you feel like a team.

You don't even have to travel off the map to find a country where English is a second (or nonexistent) language. The following are no more than a few hours from American borders:

- Mexico (Spanish)

- Central America (Spanish)

- Québec, Canada (French)

- Iceland (Icelandic)

- Caribbean (on the non-English-speaking islands, Spanish, French, or Dutch)

• S p i c e I t U p •

Buy a guidebook and spend an evening in bed reading and planning together.

4 Shed your clothes along with your inhibitions with a weekend au naturel (read "naked"). Nudist camps have grown up. These days, you can do everything in your birthday suit from exotic beach holidays to running 5k races to going to a resort to hitting the high seas on a cruise.

It may be hard to believe, but getting naked, even for a short time—especially when everyone else is also doing it—can make you feel incredibly sexy and comfortable within your skin. (Why do you think there are all those topless French beaches?) "Being a nudist isn't about being in great shape or even looking good," says John, 38, who regularly goes on nudist holidays with his wife (they leave the kids home). "It's about feeling free and having a fun time. No one is trying to impress everyone with his or her body. When everyone is naked, the person who stands out is the one who is dressed!"

Still, in case your confidence needs a boost, here are some naked tips to make you feel buff about being buff:

- Put on a self-tanner; everyone always looks better in tint. Don't do the real thing unless you think sunspots and wrinkles are sexy.

- Add a healthy sheen to your skin with a really good moisturizer.

- Slip on one eye-snagging bold accessory like a big wrist cuff or sparkly ankle bracelet to draw eyes away from your other parts.

- Put up your hair with a few tendrils hanging down. You'll feel instantly taller, sexier, and polished.

- Groom your hair down there. You don't have to get creative and make shapes. But keeping things neat and trim will make you feel less self-conscious about baring all.

Also, think: fewer clothes = less luggage = less hassle. (Who cares if the airline loses your suitcase?) And you won't have to dress up to get good service or waste time fumbling with buttons when you want to give each other good service.

Two things you do want to make sure that you pack: sunscreen and insect repellent.

5 Give your date a turbocharge and rent a sexy car for the day to tool around in.

A joyride in a Ferrari 355 Spider will run about $1,000 a day. Or reserve a Hummer and go off-roading. If you don't need that much of a rush, you could rent a Porsche 996 Cabrio for about $400 a day or a Plymouth Prowler for a little more than $300. Check out exoticcarrental.com for a directory of nationwide rental locations. For a more budget-conscious drive, take a road trip down memory lane and rent a van from your local Rent-A-Wreck and make it rock like two teenagers! One defensive driving tip: Divvy up your wheel time before you head out to avoid shotgun arguments.

To get into a cozy parking position no matter what size your vehicle, have your guy sit on the passenger side and tilt the passenger seat back as much as you can. Then sit on top of him facing the windshield, holding onto the dashboard for balance and controlling the movement. Make sure you put the emergency brake on before you start movin' and a groovin'.

• Spice It Up •

Get decked out in black leather and hire a Harley for the day.

6 Pull an all-nighter and check into the closest high-end hotel. Even if it's less than a mile from your own bed, you'll still feel transported to luxury land where the only thing you need to concentrate on is each other. For one thing, there is a great big bed. For another, there is a DO NOT DISTURB sign that actually works. Lounge in the fluffy white robes, order room service and feed each other in bed (you're not cleaning up so you don't have to worry about the crumbs), get hot in the steam room, have a randy romp in the Jacuzzi (preferably heart-shaped and in your room), and sleep until checkout.

7 If you really want to get away from it all, head about two thousand feet into the atmosphere and take a ride over your town via balloon, plane, or helicopter (packages range from $90 to $250 per person, depending on the type of flight and the extras, such as Champagne, snacks, flowers, or a limousine ride to the takeoff point).

• Spice It Up •

Some private planes offer a Mile High Flight — go to milehighclub.com/flights where you and your hubby can get it on in the comfort of your own private jet.

8 Think *Love Boat* and take a cruise to romance. Not sure if you can squeeze in a seven-day jaunt on the high seas? Royal Caribbean International, Disney Cruise Line, and Carnival Cruise Line now offer three-night mini cruises departing from various coastal cities. All your needs are completely taken care of: The food is fabulous and abundant; there is a wide choice of entertainment (including a sunrise and sunset show on the bow and deck chairs for curling up and smooching); and you'll have exotic stopovers for exploring. To really pump up the passion, splurge a little and choose a stateroom with a private balcony! Imagine the possibilities: alone on your balcony, the sun setting over the horizon, Champagne flute in hand, a warm breeze, and soft music playing. Tip: To avoid the crowds and kids, see if the cruise offers a minimum age requirement.

9 Get away from it all. One way is to head to an island. It doesn't have to be a desert island for you to feel remote from your world. Any place where the only access is via bridge, tunnel, or boat can make you feel cut off from everything but each other.

10 Bliss out at a spa. When your senses are being indulged (flower petals scattered on your bed or in the bath, air redolent with the fragrance of essential oils, and soothing music), it's easy to put your cares aside and concentrate on the here and now. And then there are the treatments. Side by side, you're slowly and gently touched and rubbed, cleansed and polished to a newer, shinier you. Check out spafinder.com for resorts that offer facilities for couples.

PICKUP DATES

No plan? No problem. Here are four last-minute dates, no forethought required.

1 Take a trip to nowhere. No packing, no planning, no idea. Just get in the car and start driving off into the sunset together.

Stop when you're hungry or thirsty. If there is an interesting sight or town, pause and explore. So much of life seems to be about staying on top of things and keeping to today's agenda. By letting go and following your heart, you'll recapture that exciting sense of the unknown you felt when you first met.

2 If you can't get away to a tropical paradise, day-trip at a botanical garden instead and frolic in the hothouse.

3 Have a hobo date. Head to the train station and hop on the first available train. Take it all the way to the end of the line if time allows, or get off at the first stop and spend the day exploring.

4 Check out the Web sites of major airlines and travel operators (like lastminutetravel.com). Most offer fabulous last-minute deals to everywhere from the mundane to the exotic. There's a place to suit every mood.

REAL-STEAL DEALS

Time away doesn't necessarily have to cost you more than a big night out on the town at home.

- These budget stays may not be just like home, but that's the point.

  I. CAMPING: State parks are usually a good deal and the nightlife is usually nothing wilder than a cricket concert. You can set up a tent, cook over an open fire, and gaze at the stars at night (see Chapter 8 for more on camping dates).

2. **CABIN RENTAL:** If you prefer your rustic break to include four walls, local lakes and camping areas have inexpensive secluded cabins, especially off-season.

3. **BED AND BREAKFAST:** Check out smaller towns for affordable B&Bs.

4. **HOTELS WITH KITCHENETTES:** If you're staying in a city, all those meals out can add up. Check into a self-sufficiency so you have more time and money for your favorite pursuits.

5. **LUXURY HOTELS:** Book during off-season and nonpeak times (such as midweek) for great deals. Making your reservation online can save even more money.

- Become a dealer. Keep your eye out for special discounts in the travel section of your local newspaper. Sunday papers often come with coupon inserts for chain restaurants that you can use while you are away.

- One-stop shop on budget travel sites like Orbitz.com, travelocity.com, mobissimo.com, and kayak.com. They have multiple instant searches for the best prices for plane trips, cruises, car rentals, and hotels.

DATING DILEMMAS

When you make all the effort to take time away, you want it to be perfect, dammit. But the fun of travel is that the unexpected can, and often does, happen. Not

knowing exactly what awaits allows so much room for wonder, amazement, and unanticipated beauty. On the other hand, uncertainty can also sometimes be frustrating, upsetting, and even scary. Here's how to act like a seasoned traveler.

Dilemma #1

The place is a dive; the weather is terrible; and the food is barely edible.

There will be delays; rooms will look different from the way they did in the pictures; rain will fall but you will still have time alone together despite it all. Keeping a great attitude is much better than letting the less-than-perfect plan ruin a great weekend. Instead of complaining, think of how you will retell this as a funny story once you get home.

Dilemma #2

You have a fight.

You occasionally say a sharp word or two or have a disagreement at home. You will on the road, too. Vacations are funny things. We take them because we need to relax, but they're pretty high on the list of events that cause people the most stress; and worst of all, it's all documented in snapshots. That's because fears, anxieties, and eccentric behavior can show up on a trip, blossoming out of control from the hustle of airports, the irritation of delayed flights, or the monotony of driving. That doesn't mean the trip, even if it's a once-in-a-lifetime thing, was spoiled. It does, however, mean there is an opportunity for great makeup sex. Just remember to always ask for directions when lost (you'll get to the hotel room much faster that way).

Dilemma #3
You're not having sex 24/7.

The fact that this is supposed to be a love trip can put tremendous pressure on you. You think, "We're by ourselves at this beautiful spot and we should be having sex." Except that it's on vacations that sex problems often become apparent. If you've lost your desire, it may not be so obvious in your busy daily life. But when you have nothing to do but enjoy each other, it can feel painfully personal if one of you is not in the mood. Take heart. Even though you know each other's bodies intimately, it doesn't mean that your libidos are automatically going to go *cha-ching* just because you've managed to finagle some guaranteed naked downtime together. Try this: Instead of focusing so much on the specific act of making beautiful sheet music together, focus on making the melody of love: talking and laughing together, holding hands, stealing kisses as you walk arm in arm. This is what foreplay really is: connecting and reconnecting with each other.

Dilemma #4
You can't do everything you wanted to do.

Squelch any camp-counselor tendencies and let the day play out at a relaxed pace. Even if you have a whole list of places you want to see, save time to sit at a café, slowly sip a drink, and do nothing but savor each other's company and your surroundings.

Dilemma #5
You couldn't park the kids.

This does not mean your romantic getaway now has to be rerouted to waiting in line for three hours at Disney. Many hotels and resorts offer kids' programs and sitting to give you some free love time. (Not for nothing is the kids' club in some resorts dubbed the Nookie Club!)

But be aware. Since child-care licensing laws and requirements vary from state to state, country to country, there is no regulatory board that oversees the services offered by every hotel around the world. Your best bet for finding out who is watching the kids is to start by contacting hotels and inquiring about its individual services.

Ask the same questions you'd ask your own babysitter or local day-care center. Check the credentials of the employees in charge of watching the children. Are they licensed child-care providers or hotel staff members? Also note the ratio of kids to adults. When traveling internationally, it's also important to make sure that you and the caregivers speak the same language so there are no communication problems. Remember, you can never ask too many questions when it comes to your children's safety.

Chapter 11

DOUBLE
DATERS

Being part of a couple may not mean you never have to say you're sorry, but it does mean that you always have a date for Saturday night. Hooray! Except dating doesn't have to be an exclusive affair. True, the whole idea behind date night is about getting some quality one-on-one time with your mate. But, occasionally, you need to spread the love around and invite others on your outing.

When we think of intimacy, we think we can't get too much of a good thing. But you really can't have all of your needs met by one person. The longest-lasting, brightest-burning marriages are those that recognize that spending time with people other than your partner doesn't take away from the state of your union; it enriches it. Group dating helps startle your romance awake by exposing you to new ideas and interests. "A group of us recently had a date at an amusement park. It never would have occurred to me that we could have fun going on rides without our kids along, but it was a hoot," says Anne, 45. "And there was no whining over waiting in lines or being thirsty or having to go to the bathroom." But that excitement and sense of possibility is only a small part of the group date's value. Seeing your partner in action outside the day-to-day of building a life together reminds you that he is more than that sweet but predictable guy who can be counted on to fall asleep while watching the evening news. He's actually kind of witty and charming and—gasp!—sexy.

Read on for how to gather a crowd on your next night out.

TEN MUST-DO DATES FOR WHEN THE GANG'S ALL HERE

It doesn't take much effort to increase the number of people on your date. Try these trysts when you want to enjoy the company of good friends.

1 Organize a tasting night. What you sample is up to you: It could be top-end chocolate, cheap wine, foreign beers, exotic fruits, coffee from different countries, or whatever your palate fancies. Each person or couple brings enough of whatever the night's theme is to share around (get them to check in with you so there are no duplications). If you want to make it a regular event, taste products from a specific region or style each time. Provide each guest with a glass of water for palate cleansing between tastes and a pen and paper for note taking.

2 Call up your favorite lovebirds. You know, the ones you usually avoid because it's annoying to spend the evening with a couple who is so crazy in love that neither one can keep his or her hands off the other. Instead of resenting their glow, try letting a little of it rub off on you. Sexual energy can be contagious. The key is to participate in their love play rather than just watch it. So get together for drinks or dinner instead of a movie or show so you can relax, converse, and let loose.

• Spice It Up •

Steam up your mood before you even meet up by indulging in a little touch and tease pre-play as you get ready to go out. Deep, passionate kisses, a hand cupping a bottom, a tongue tickling an ear won't just get your blood pumping (a requisite for exquisite toe curls), they're tantalizing promises of what will come later.

3 Make a date with a couple you don't know that well. It will have the delicious anxiety and thrill of a first romantic date (except it's with four people and you go home with someone you are already sleeping with). To relieve the getting-to-know-you awkwardness, organize the date around an activity like golfing or bowling. This way, you can still talk and have something to talk about (and possibly laugh about,) like your unerring ability to always land the ball in the sandpit or gutter.

4 Host a theme dinner. While it's always fun to get together with the gang for a laugh and a nosh, centering your meal around a theme adds a fresh feel to your get-together. Here are some ideas to party on:

- **THE SIMPSONS DINNER PARTY:** Each couple brings a dish loved by America's most famous dysfunctional family. Up the ante by asking people to dress in character.

- **MURDER MYSTERY:** Everyone plays a part. See who can solve the mystery first. (There are kits available for around $30 to help you plan things. Search for "murder mystery parties" online).

- **MEXICAN FIESTA:** Combine margaritas with a piñata, and you have everything you need for a hot, hot night.

- **BIZARRO FIFTIES DINNER:** The men do all the cooking and cleaning up.

- **TEXAS BBQ:** Think big!

- **CREATE A COCKTAIL CLUB:** Take a break from pizza and Cokes with a sophisticated soiree. Wear swanky clothes, have Frank Sinatra CDs playing in the background, and get set to flirt and mingle.

5 Host a cocktail brunch. Serve mini French toasts, silver-dollar pancakes, and juice-infused cocktails. Brew up a load of coffee and crank up classical tunes or some morning jazz to set the morning mood.

Here, are five classic cocktails you'll need to know how to mix to get your party shaking. Each recipe makes one cocktail.

• Cosmopolitan •

1½ ounces (lemon-infused) vodka
½ ounce Cointreau
1 ounce cranberry juice
¼ ounce Freshly squeezed lemon or lime
  juice
Twist of lemon

Stir or shake vodka, Cointreau, cranberry juice, and lemon juice with ice and strain into a chilled martini glass. Garnish with a twist of lemon.

• Dry Martini •

2½ ounces dry gin
½ ounce dry vermouth
1 green olive or twist of lemon

Stir gin and vermouth with ice. Strain into a chilled martini glass. Garnish with a green olive or twist of lemon.

• Margarita •

1½ ounces tequila
½ ounces Cointreau or Triple Sec
1 ounce lime juice
Salt

Shake and strain tequila, Cointreau, and lime juice
into a large cocktail glass rimmed with salt.

• Tom Collins •

2 ounces gin
1 ounce lemon juice
1 teaspoon sugar
3 ounces club soda
1 slice orange and 1 maraschino cherry

In a cocktail shaker half-filled with ice cubes, combine the gin, lemon juice, and sugar. Shake well.
Strain into a highball glass almost filled with ice
cubes. Add the club soda. Stir and garnish with the
orange slice and cherry.

• Whiskey Sour •

2 ounces whiskey
1½ tablespoons lemon juice
½ teaspoon powdered sugar
Maraschino cherries
½ slice lemon

Shake and strain whiskey, lemon juice, and sugar
into a rocks glass. Garnish with a red cherry and a
lemon slice.

When you know your friends' habits and quirks as well as you know your partner's, it's time to add new blood to your group. Invite at least two couples no one has ever met before to your next group event, and make sure you break up couples so no couples sit next to each other.

6 Throw yourself a kiddy birthday party. Put all the same creative energy you throw into your children's big-day bashes into one for yourself: Send invitations, book some entertainment, blow up balloons (see balloonhq.com for instructions on how to twist them into funny shapes), serve a birthday cake with enough candles to represent your age (plus one for next year), and give out goody bags at the end of the party. Or pile everyone into the minivan for an off-site party at the movie theater, skating rink, or bowling alley.

• S p i c e   I t   U p •

Make it a dance party. Mix a playlist of tunes from the year you were born with your usual picks.

7 Certain types of entertainment seem to be more fun when you go to them en masse:

- See if there is a Mystery Dinner in your area. You eat while watching a murder-mystery play and have to guess "who dun it" by dessert.

- If you want a night practically guaranteed to end in giggles, check out a comedy club (many serve meals before the show). But make sure you find out the type of humor on offer before you go, or you may end up listening to "The definition of a wife is an attachment you screw on the bed to get the housework done" jokes. Ha-ha.

- Find a local karaoke bar you can all meet at, or take turns hosting your own out-of-tune serenade. (You can rent a portable karaoke machine for around $50 from a music supply store or download cheesy ballads straight from karaoke.oddcast.com or karaoke com.) If the only place you ever sing is the shower, you'll be surprised how exhilarating it feels to belt it out in public (and stay dry).

• Spice It Up •

Croon a classic love song, locking eyes with your partner for the entire tune.

8 Re-create those schedule-free-anything-can-happen heady days of college by organizing a night out at a pool hall. Or head to a local dive bar and kick back and relax over a pitcher of beer (pitching quarters, anyone?).

9 Rally a group of weekend warriors to take part in an event like a bike-a-thon, a run, or a walk-a-thon. Working in a group means you can all train together and cheerlead each other as needed. Make sure you order up some matching Tees to wear on the day. There are also some triathlons that let you switch off competitors for each event, letting you put your best sports foot forward. (See usatriathlon.org for more info.)

10 Pool your resources. Rent a boat for your own private dinner/dancing cruise. Or book a hall for the night and plan a fifties-style sock hop. (Make sure you bring a bottle to spin and have some dark corners just for necking.) Or divide yourselves into teams and play a raucous game of volleyball (use water balloons instead of a real ball). You might be able to even reserve your local amusement park, go-kart track, or water slide during off hours.

PICKUP DATES

No plan? No problem. Here are four last-minute group dates, no forethought required.

1 Lighten your load by turning something that smacks of "gotta do" into something you want to do. For instance, turn your daughter's soccer game into a brunch date with some of the other parents there by bringing bagels and a Thermos of hot drink. Or make a lunch date with your posse to meet on a weekend at the playground so the kids can play while you dally over sandwiches and iced frappuccinos.

2 Tired of meeting friends at a restaurant? Try throwing an impromptu dinner party-cum-Iron Chef cooking class. Everyone raids his or her refrigerator, and then you all work together to create a feast with the bounty.

3 Play outside. E-mail half a dozen friends or so and invite them to take a hike or play a game of Frisbee, golf, or flag football.

4 It's hard enough trying to coordinate your own schedule to get out at night, let alone four or ten of your nearest and dearests' itineraries. So be less ambitious and get together for part of an evening. Pick a movie and a restaurant to go to and then throw the times of your reservation and film out to the general crowd. That way, your friends can choose when they can join you. Just don't pick a restaurant that can't accommodate a crowd if everyone shows up!

REAL-STEAL DEALS

These value deals are a good bet for when everyone is on a different budget.

- Group get-togethers are the warehouse stores of dating. Because you're doing things in bulk, the cost is lower. Bus trips, tour or museum entrance fees, amusement parks, theaters, bowling alleys, ski resorts, cinemas, and even some restaurants often offer group discounts if you can guarantee a minimum of people (usually around twenty). However, it helps if everyone pays up front so no one gets left holding the bill.

- Have a swap meet/ice cream social where participants bring an item and take a different item in exchange. Keep things simple with trading themes: books, kids' outerwear, toys, sports equipment, and so on. Ask everyone to bring an ice cream sundae ingredient (such as ice cream, toppings, and whipped cream). Shopping has never seemed so sweet.

- Instead of a book club, start a music club. Every get-together, have participants bring a favorite CD to spin and talk about why these tunes move them. Depending on the type of beat, everyone can then get down and start dancing, or, if it's more like background music, talking the night away.

- Dig out your favorite group board games and invite friends over for a night of fun. Jessica, 28, says because she and her husband don't have much money for a night on the town, they started picking up games at garage sales. "At first, just the two of us played. But we had friends over for dinner one night and discovered the fun of competing with other people. Sometimes it's every person on their own or else we play in teams: the girls against the guys or couples against couples. I think we have more fun than if we just went out somewhere on a regular date night, and it is certainly a lot cheaper. We all pitch in for a big pasta dinner and one of those big bottles of wine."

- Start with familiar games like Scrabble, Pictionary, Twister, Clue, and Bunko so you don't get bogged down going over the rules. But whatever game you end up playing, be warned: Different personalities come out when the competitive juices start going. According to research, you can learn more about someone by playing a game than by going on ten dates. And you can learn more about yourself by playing a game than you can from several therapy sessions.

  In addition to the old favorites, pick up these five board games to keep the fun going in your playdates (available from online outlets like boardsandbits.com, funagain.com, and gamefest.com):

1. **SAN JUAN:** Every card in the game depicts a building that you can construct in the Puerto Rican capital. But there's a Donald Trump twist that requires you to make tough decisions: to pay for a building you must discard cards from your hand.

2. **TIME'S UP:** Players compete over three rounds of increasing difficulty to identify the same set of celebrities. It's not as easy as it sounds, but it'll have you in stitches.

3. **APPLES TO APPLES:** A mad-lib matching game of adjectives and nouns.

4. **BEYOND BALDERDASH:** Making up definitions for unusual words is the basis for this game. Expanding on the original Balderdash, categories now include words, people, initials, dates, and movie plots. Best bluffer wins.

5. **FIB OR NOT?:** Players take turns telling stories in various categories (e.g., "an embarrassing moment"). If you can convince other players that your true stories are false and vice versa, you're well on the way to winning.

DATING DILEMMAS

Double dating seems like it's going to be easy and fun, but things can get really complicated really quickly. Insecurities, weirdness, touchy issues, and even attractions can crop up with four people as easily as with two. Here's how to sidestep any doubles troubles.

Dilemma #1
One half of your foursome doesn't like the evening's program.

While you can't please everyone all of the time, you should be able to figure out something to do that works for all of you. If someone nay-says everything suggested, then it's probably a good indication that you do not make winning doubles partners.

Dilemma #2
You ended up spending the car payment on dinner.

Make sure that the plans are within everyone's budget. And if you are going out for a meal, either ask for separate checks before you order or accept the fact that the meal may be split down the middle even though you chose less expensive entrees or didn't drink as much.

Dilemma #3
Some of your party feels left out.

A date can turn into an exclusive evening when two of you have a connection that the other two don't share. Perhaps you're old girlfriends bringing your mates to meet, or they're colleagues at work. While there will (and should) be some moments when you're conversing in two's, it should never be about something the other people can't directly relate or contribute to. No one should feel completely left out of the table talk.

Dilemma #4
You forgot to make a code.

Your match may not be made in heaven after all. In which case, you might want to cut the evening short. Or it could be that your partner is about to put his or her foot in it about some top-secret tidbit that you shouldn't have but did pass on about one of the people you are out with. Have a prearranged signal, like using a phrase that you never use (for instance, saying "I have to go to the little girl's room" when you always call it the restroom), to let your partner know that you want to wrap the evening up or that it's time to change the subject (fast!).

Dilemma #5
The other couple is having a fight night.

It's hard enough dealing with your own marital discord; the last thing you want to be privy to is someone else's dirty laundry. Don't get pulled into their drama, even if it's perfectly obvious to you who is right and who is wrong, even if you know in another life you could have been Judge Judy. Make like Switzerland and stay neutral. If it turns into a shouting match, call it a night (make sure you leave your share of the check before leaving). Chances are, they will be so wrapped up in their battle, they won't even notice that you're gone.

If you're the ones getting bent out of shape, excuse yourselves and go somewhere private to talk, whether it's outside or by the restrooms. Then decide fast: Can you both put this on hold and have a semigood night? If you sense that you really can't, call it a night.

Dilemma #6
The other couple is groping each other and engaging in baby talk.

You know better than to slip your guy a little tongue between courses (right?), but it's trickier (and grosser) when your "dates" are doing it. Try a light-hearted, "Gee, you must have not seen each other in a long time." If they don't get the hint, they will if you nudge your man and say, "Hey, free porn!"

Dilemma #7
They don't seem interested in a rematch.

It happens. Maybe you aren't their type or they have decided that they only have time for dating each other. Let it go. Don't stalk them. Somewhere out there, there is your soul mate couple.

Dilemma #8
You are not the Brady Bunch.

Just because you want everyone to get along and love each other doesn't mean it will happen. It could be a case of different interests, or it may be that one member of the party is simply an intolerable ass. However, just because some of you aren't bonding, it doesn't mean you can't be civil to each other. Politics, religion, and sex are the three forbidden topics of polite conversation. If things are getting hairy, stick with sex and stay mum about the other two.

Dilemma #9

The other woman is flirting outrageously with your honey.

Or her partner is making goo-goo eyes at you. Or your guy is the one out of line. Or you are. Cool things down by lovingly caressing your partner's arm and purring to the group at large, "I'm afraid we have to leave now as we want to go home and make crazy love."

If it was your guy who was wolf-whistling, you can give him his warning card once you're out of earshot of the other couple. Even if he is a natural-born flirt, he shouldn't make you feel uncomfortable with his, *ahem,* friendliness. However, aim for a win-win resolution. Say that a little low-key flirting is fine as long as he directs some of his banter in your direction and he ravishes you that night.

Chapter 12

THE BIG DATES

There are dates and then there are the Big Four: birthdays, special anniversaries, New Year's Eve, and the mother of all lovers' days, Valentine's Day. Yeah, yeah, yeah, you know that true romance, the kind that brings you to deeper levels of devotion and trust, is really in the heartfelt daily expressions of love: the spontaneous back rubs, the for-no-particular-reason bouquet of flowers, the coffee already made when you get up in the morning, the sweet "thinking-of-you" mid-afternoon e-mails, the surprise cupcakes picked up on the way home, the unexpected compliment lobbed your way, and the other countless things that you (hopefully) do for each other on a regular basis. But if you don't manage to squeeze in some quality couple's time on an ordinary day, you're probably not going to get too bent out of shape. If you can't find that quality time on one of the Big Four Dates, *ay-yi-yi.*

Those sorts of built-in expectations can place a tremendous amount of pressure for everything to be just right on those dates. But any kind of romantic overload can make you forget what you are meant to celebrate (hint: your love for each other). Read on for some bang-up ways to capture the moment (no stress involved).

TEN MUST-DO DATES BECAUSE THEY'RE MARKED IN RED ON YOUR CALENDAR (AT LEAST THEY SHOULD BE)

Because these happy occasions happen just once a year, you want to make the most of them.

• Valentine's Day •

This day is so much more than flowers and chocolates. It's about rejoicing and reflecting on your love for each other. Surprisingly, sharing a smile is a huge part of that. Humor, as many psychotherapists have observed, is the superglue that keeps you bonded. When a couple can giggle and have fun together, it's often a signal that there is loads of joy in their marriage, which, in turn, helps them laugh instead of fight through the bumpy

times. So skip the fancy-dinner-with-good-bottle-of-wine, and yuck-yuck your way through one of these nights on the town instead:

1 Say "cheese." When was the last time you were both in a photo at the same time? Even if it was more recently than your wedding, chances are, the majority of your postvow snaps have one of you posing solo in front of some monument or en masse with the kids. Make a date with a photographer for a fancy shot of the two of you in a tight clinch. You can make it glam and dress up in fancy clothes, or go with a romantic theme (think soft lighting and a pink gauzy backdrop). Or simply head into a photo booth. "We always take goofy photo-booth pictures when we go out together," says one woman. "Then we paste them in their own album. It's fun, and sometimes illuminating, to look back over them. For instance, the snap taken a few months after our son was born. I may remember life being really stressed and feeling like we weren't communicating really well, but then I'll look at our date photo from that time and see that even though things were really hard, the picture shows how much joy and love we were also feeling."

2 Indulge your inner child. Head to your local toy store and pick out a toy that you can play with together. Maybe it's something you always wanted as a kid. Throw in a couple of bubble bottles and a bucket of sidewalk chalk for a fun-'n'-games night.

3 For a sweet evening out with zero calories, croon saccharine love songs to each other at a karaoke bar.

4 The love tokens you exchange on Valentine's Day have the power to make or break your date. Skip the golf gloves he'll never wear and the heart-shaped Russell Stover chocolate boxes. Instead, here's how to put a smile on your faces.

- Put a smile on your face first thing in the morning. Get matching mugs customized with a favorite family saying (google "custom mugs"). "We quote Monty Python to get each other to laugh at serious moments," says Renee, 31. "So for Valentine's Day, I got two mugs inscribed with 'Nobody expects the Spanish Inquisition!'"

- Chocolates are a sweet nothing. Bypass the usual shrink-wrapped heart. A stack of favorite movies that you have seen together bundled together with a ribbon will have the same sweet effect. But if you do want to say it with chocolates, create your own whimsical love message: At mms.com you can write your own mini love ditty to be printed on M&Ms, while personalizedsweets.com will inscribe anything from candy bars and hearts to keepsake tins.

- Don't show your love with a store-bought card. Scrapbook it instead. Dig up those saved bits of relationship memorabilia (the ticket stub from the first movie you went to, the menu from your first romantic meal, the old photos that didn't make it into the album, the first love note you sent each other, and even old cards you sent to each other), and make a date to organize them into a book of memories. Your dig into the past is sure to make you laugh and smile as you recall your life together. You can purchase the book, background paper, stickers, and other supplies from any craft store.

- Color your love. If scrapbooking isn't your thing, there's another alternative to Hallmark: Pick up a silly coloring book and fill it in together. When you're done, you can tear out your collaboration and then sign and frame it.

- Eat alone. Your romantic dinner *à deux* can feel crowded when you are crammed in with a dozen other couples celebrating their love. Use the home-field advantage and pick up a meal of fun gourmet finger foods: mini quiches, egg rolls, frozen hors d'oeuvres, and chocolate-dipped fruits. He'll be eating out of your hand all night.

• Your Anniversary •

One of the sweetest things about anniversaries is that they give you a chance to celebrate your union over and over and to travel down memory lane together.

1 Relationship memories are the story of your love life together. They tell of the obstacles you may have overcome and reveal the connection you had before the two of you might even have been aware of it. Flash back to those early feelings with these dates down memory lane.

- Relive your first date. If possible, follow the same itinerary and include as many of the same details as possible. Even though you know how it ends, recalling how you talked, explored, and began your lifelong journey of getting to know each other can remind you that there is still much to learn not only about each other but also about yourselves and your marriage.

- Go back to your future. Remember how, when you first fell in love, you both only saw the best about each other and focused on how wonderful you both were ("He's so strong, he can run ten miles. Sigh")? As time goes by, you start to lose the feelings from that exciting, mysterious early phase of your relationship. Refreshing your memory puts you back in the moment when your heart would start thumping just at the thought of spending time together and makes you aware of how your love has deepened and matured since those days. Go back to the cinema where you used to catch the double Hitchcock features while sharing a pack of Twizzlers, knock on the door of your first apartment and ask to have a look around, seek out the restaurant where he proposed to you, revisit the park where the geese stole your romantic picnic (and remember to bring his sneakers).

- Take up an old hobby again. Everyone has a "couple's thing," something they used to do together all the time that somehow got edged out by the demands of work and family. It's time to dust off your dueling banjos, dig out your bowling shoes, buy a season ticket to your local theater rep, or whatever you need to do to rekindle your old interests. Reminding your-self of the things you used to feel passionate about as a couple can make you feel passionate about each other now.

- Take a lesson in Love 101 and have a college-style date: It feels like you have all day, and your biggest worry is getting to class on time the following after-noon. Grab a blanket and a Thermos of something you need an I.D. to buy and huddle together at a local college football game, or get yourself in a sweaty lather dancing the night away to a local bar band, or split a bottle of cheap vino and a bowl of peanuts at the neighborhood dive, or hold hands and talk for hours over a single order of fries at some hole-in-the-wall restaurant (but this time leave a good tip); or go to a party and pretend to pick each other up.

2 Get grooving. You're never too ancient to catch your favorite classic rock band (except now it's called "easy listen-ing!") on its reunion tour. Or hit a local cover band that plays music from the days when you were dating. "Every August I score tickets to an outdoor concert," says one woman. "I don a concert T-shirt from our dating days and dance wildly, just like I did on our first date."

3 Renew your matrimonial vows. You don't have to wait until you've been bonded for fifty years (and the wedding dress no longer fits) before confirming that you'd get hitched all over again. Unlike an actual wedding, there are far fewer dos and don'ts about vow renewal. You can whisper your eternal love to each other under a starry night or make a big party of it. Do it at home or head to a popular wedding destination. Disneyland, Las Vegas, Hawaii, and cruise trips are the top sites for getting rehitched. (Maybe you didn't want Goofy or Elvis to marry you the first time, but the second? Go for it.) Repeat the vows you already made or write new ones more relevant to your lives today. Either way, get ready for some wedding-night fun.

• Spice It Up •

You don't need to wait for him to get down on one knee. Go ahead and propose to him, complete with a ring. (Buy new bands specially engraved or make your own out of a pipe cleaner and a bead.)

4 Dedicate an extra anniversary (or two). Why restrict the only hullabaloo of your coupledom to one measly day a year? The date that you met, the date that you had your first official date, the date that you first "invited him up for coffee," the date that you first said you loved each other, the date that you got engaged, the date that you met each other's parents or best friends or pets are all worthy of a special celebration. "Not long after I started 'hanging out' with my wife, the number 1111 began to show up everywhere from clocks (11:11) to invoices, phone numbers, license plates, even our order number for our pizza. I even proposed at 11:11 P.M. (we didn't realize until after she had said yes!)," says Robert, 39. "Then we found out that it's a Buddhist belief to do what makes you happiest at eleven-eleven. Naturally, we try and make the eleventh of the month our special night out and make sure that we really have a big celebration on November 11!"

5 To mark the occasion, here are five sexy gifts you can give one another:

1. A sexual free-for-all that lasts longer than your last fight.

2. A schedule on which you both go to bed and get up at the same time at least once a week.

3. At least one night spent on a vibrating bed or one session using a sex toy.

4. A secret that only the two of you know.

5. A list of things you want to do together. Try to update it at least once a year.

• Your Birthdays •

Birthdays are your own personal special day, and as such they deserve a big celebration. A birthday acknowledges your soul-mate qualifications. You are like no other person alive, no person who has ever lived, and no person who will ever live will. So go out and eat cake.

1 It's your birthday, but if planning special occasions isn't in your guy's bag of talents, don't sweat it. It's better to have a fun time than stew all day because you know he isn't going to deliver. Hand him a list of everything you want to have happen on your special day. Make it as detailed as you feel you need to, from your present to the phone numbers of the people with whom you want to celebrate. (You know the man. How much direction does he feel comfortable with?)

2 It's his birthday, but forget the party. Instead, the following man-friendly outings will keep him crazy in love (and gratefully reciprocating when your day rolls around).

- Test-drive a fun sports car.

- Make a surprise visit to an adult toy store. Tell him he can buy whatever he wants to use at a play date that night.

- Rent him a Harley for an afternoon of easy riding.

- Head to a batting cage and swing at some balls.

- Hit a sports bar and cheer on his team.

- Plan a poker night (up the ante and make it strip poker).

- Get tickets to see his favorite team play in spring training.

- Suit up for a day playing paintball or laser tag.

- Make him a romantic he-man dinner: Cook him up a hunking slab of USDA prime meat (the best cut is porterhouse because it's part filet and part sirloin, so you get two super-rich cuts in one) and serve it with a baked potato and beer.

- If you know he would give an eyetooth to see his team play, snag a pair of tickets for primo seats.

3 If you're not sports savvy, you can make his day even more just-for-him memorable by mastering the secrets to his inner-man world.

- Learn the lingo: Every sport has its own secret language. To start speaking like the locals in a jiffy (which, let's face it, is the most time you have to devote to this stuff anyway), see moms guide.com for the basics, rules, and phrases used in the more popular sports, or else look up specific sports in one of the *Dummies* or *Complete Idiot* series.

- Become a cardsharp. Even if you have no interest in sitting down with the boys for a night of brewskis and Dagwoods, mastering the basics of Texas Hold'em (the most popular type of poker) assures that you won't be the only one in your birthday suit the next time you play strip poker. See pokersyte.com to get you started on the fundamentals of the game.

- Give him the shaft and learn to play darts. According to Dr. Darts, who has a few throwing trophies under his belt, throwing a dart is not that different from throwing a ball: You aim, pull your arm backward, push your arm forward, let go, and (here's the sell to every successful pitch) follow-through.

- Break his balls and learn to play pool. You don't need a lot of force to make the break in pool. You just hit that first ball where it counts. "The biggest mistake people make is aiming for the center of the ball," says Larry aka "Fast Larry" Guninger, holder of the record for sinking the most balls in one break (eight for you sports-trivia whonks). Instead, he advises you to find the dot of light on the first ball (caused by the overhead light). Hit it and watch the balls scatter. Check out more tips at fastlarrypool.com.

• New Year's Eve •

The end of a year is a good time to pause and appreciate what you have accomplished together and where you want to go next.

1 Conjure up your marriage's passionate roots and pull out your old love letters. Even though you may have changed since then, rereading them will spark memories of your first attraction and make you realize how far you have come together.

• Spice It Up •

Save time to write new love letters. Spell out, in unashamed mushy detail, what you adore about and value in each other. Include how you hope your relationship will continue to grow and strengthen in the coming year.

2 Start the new year with a bang. Make a resolution that doesn't feel like hard work to keep: more and better sex this year, for example. The following get-closer strategies will keep you up well past midnight madness.

- Stop neglecting your lips. Often overlooked as mere roadblocks to the vagina, the labia are packed with nerve endings and are not to be ignored by his hands and lips.

- Get out of the missionary. The best position for hitting the G-spot is for him to enter you doggy style from the rear and, keeping his hands on your hips, to pull you toward him each time he thrusts forward.

- Learn just one move from the *Kama Sutra.*

- Don't wait for him to please you; go after your own pleasure. You're a committed couple: you've seen each other in every state of undress; he's possibly seen you push out a baby or two—it's time that you tell (or at least show) him exactly how you like being touched and encourage him to be your pleasure guide to his body.

- Accept the fact that your hormones generally take longer to wake up than his. So stop trying to keep to his pace. Instead, ask him to slow down to yours.

PICKUP DATES

No plan? No problem. Here are four last-minute dates, no forethought required.

1 FOR YOUR ANNIVERSARY: Tote your old photo albums to a place where you can curl up and reminisce about how much fun your life together has been. Talk about memories of your first date, your favorite times together, and what you most love about each other. Or unearth your school yearbooks and swap high school-from-hell stories. Find out at last one thing about each other from those years that you didn't know before.

2 FOR VALENTINE'S DAY: Have a good-time date. Tonight, make it a special point to talk about the good stuff in your relationship. Name at least three things that you appreciate and enjoy about being together.

3 FOR EITHER OF YOUR BIRTHDAYS: Skip the grown-up evening making polite small talk with friends and family. Head first to a favorite store where the birthday person can pick out his or her own present and over to a bakery to select a cake. Then return home for a private party.

4 FOR NEW YEAR'S EVE: Instead of focusing on saying good-bye to the old year, make a commitment to your future: Spend the date putting together a time capsule about your dating days to open ten years from now.

REAL-STEAL DEALS

True romance doesn't have to cost a thing as long as it comes from the heart.

- Journal together. If you don't always have the connecting time you would like or need, take turns each week writing down your experiences and the feelings you want to share. Then make a date to read your entries together.

- Spend the night in bed making your own sweet romance. These five little moves are sure to hit all your "gee" spots:

1. Moan. Groan. Purr. Sometimes showing your partner how mind-blowingly good he makes you feel can be the sexiest gift of all.

2. Look at each other. The tendency is to close eyes while making love, but keeping your eyes locked when you kiss, when you touch, when you join bodies makes it a more intimate experience.

3. Don't talk unless it's a murmur of love.

4. Discover a new part of his body to stroke.

5. Come back together. Keep connecting, even after the earth moves. Stay in position with your legs wrapped around each other and kiss.

DATING DILEMMAS

Your expectations are naturally high when it comes to celebrating the Big Four. Fine and dandy; hope is the thing with feathers that perches on the soul. But also be aware that just as naturally, this is a perfect setup for things to go wrong.

Dilemma #1
The celebration feels false and forced.

Even if you're a hopeless romantic, it can still feel hyped up when sentimentality is penciled in on the calendar. But being romantic isn't just about drippy candles and hearts; it's also about being adventurous. So cut the sap and try swimming naked under a full moon, hiking up a tall mountain, taking a scuba lesson together at your local pool, or challenging your-selves with a new sexual adventure—all sure to give you a romantic high.

Dilemma #2

He forgot.

Or you did. Or you both did. As long as it's a once-in-a-while thing, then in no way does it mean that you don't love each other anymore. It just means you are really, really busy. Luckily, the calendar is chockablock with potentially roman-tic substitutes.

- **JANUARY 1:** Kissing Day (some Native Americans celebrated the New Year by exchanging kisses)

- **APRIL 2:** On this day in 1725, Casanova was born

- **APRIL 28:** Officially designated as Kiss Your Mate Day

- **MAY 1-31:** Officially designated as Date Your Mate Month

- **JUNE 3:** On this day in 1936, love conquered all when the Duke of Windsor, in a famous romantic sacrifice, stepped down from the British throne to marry divorced American "commoner" Mrs. Wallis Simpson

- **AUGUST 9:** Officially designated as National Hand-Holding Day

- **AUGUST 25:** Officially designated as Kiss and Make Up Day

- **THANKSGIVING**: Make it a celebration of all you are thankful for in your relationship.

Dilemma #3
You hated the date he planned or vice versa.

Okay, so going to a sports bar so he can watch the playoffs while still going out with you is not your idea of a romantic anniversary. Temper your candor with kindness. Don't dispense with gratitude and appreciation. Say "thank you" for sharing his passion with you and then gently suggest that the next time he plans a date, he should check out the playing schedule so he doesn't feel conflicted. You can avoid future disappointment by planning together the next time one of the Big Four rolls around.

Dilemma #4
The gift was so off the mark that just the thought of it ruined your entire evening.

"My husband once gave me lacey socks—not lingerie but socks!—plus a purple marble egg and a basket of fruit for our anniversary," exclaims Linda, 32, still outraged at the memory. "He had also planned a really nice night out at our favorite restaurant, but all I could focus on and talk about was his weird gift." Turns out there was no hidden message; he had just bought her things that he thought she would like. Which is why the maxim "It's the thought that counts" especially holds true at these times.

Still, while the rational part of you knows that gifts are just that, an offering of love (often bought under duress of money or time or taste), it can be hard not to jump to the conclusion that they are a comment on your relationship. To avoid this quagmire, try giving each other these relationship gifts (although they're priceless, they won't cost you a penny).

- **THE GIFT OF LISTENING:** But you must really listen. Don't interrupt, don't daydream, don't plan your response. Just listen.

- **THE GIFT OF AFFECTION:** Be generous with appropriate hugs, kisses, pats on the back, and hand-holds. Let these small actions demonstrate the love you have for each other.

- **THE GIFT OF LAUGHTER:** Clip cartoons. Share articles and funny stories. Your gift will say "I love to laugh with you."

- **THE GIFT OF A FAVOR:** Every day, go out of your way to do something kind.

- **THE GIFT OF A COMPLIMENT:** A simple and sincere "You look great in red," "You did an amazing job," or "That was a wonderful meal" can make your partner's day.

keep the Date

There you have it. More dates than you can possibly manage in a lifetime of bliss. Now here's one last point to remember: This is a lifelong thing, with frequent refresher courses required (so keep this book handy). Sure, it takes effort. All things worthwhile do. Which is why love is an undertaking as well as a gift.

You may feel too tired to keep your date; keep it anyway. You don't have to do anything more energetic than hold each other on the couch all night. What you do isn't as important as that you do it together.

You may not feel in a romantic mood. So be it. You don't have to feel romantic. You just need to spend time together, and in time the rest will follow.

There's not enough time to be together. Make the time. Make it a point to know each other's schedule and daily rhythm. Find out where the blank spots are; even if they're only fifteen minutes, that's one-quarter of an hour together that you didn't have before. Add that up to four blank spots per day waiting to be filled, and it becomes a lot of time to connect.

Ultimately, *dating* is really just a catch-all word for *connecting, communicating, cooperating, communing* and all the other good stuff that defines a good relationship, the kind in which "happily ever after" isn't just a line out of a fairy tale. No matter what happens, ever, between you, you can rely on your dates to bring you back to the beginning of your relationship and forward into the future.

So . . . What do you want to do tonight?

index

Also available from REDBOOK
wherever books are sold.

No matter how demanding life gets, there should always be
time for amazing sex. *Love Your Sex Life!*, by Lisa Sussman,
shows you how to seize the moment, push the "hot button,"
and keep the erotic energy set on high.